CYBERSECURITY

A Cybersecurity Guidebook for
IT Security Newbies
and Professionals

MICHAEL J. HARRISON

TABLE OF CONTENTS

TABLE OF CONTENTS ii

CHAPTER ONE 1

INTRODUCTION TO CYBERSECURITY 1

    WHAT IS CYBERSECURITY? 2

    WHAT'S CYBERCRIME? 4

        CYBERCRIME AGAINST INDIVIDUAL 5
        CYBERCRIME AGAINST THE PROPERTY 7
        CRIME AGAINST GOVERNMENT 8
        CYBERCRIME AGAINST THE SOCIETY 9

    TYPES OF CYBERCRIME 10

    WHO ARE CYBERCRIMINALS? 11

    MOTIVATION FOR CYBERCRIMINALS 11

    Money 12

        Competition 12
        Political Purpose 13

    FIGs (Fun, Ideology, Grudge) 13

    Others 13

    THE KEY CONCEPT OF CYBER SECURITY 14

        Confidentiality 14
        Integrity 15
        Availability 15

    CONCEPT OF CYBERSPACE 16

    THREATS AND ATTACKS IN CYBERSECURITY 17

        CYBER THREATS 17

CHAPTER TWO 20

CYBERSECURITY FRAMEWORK 20

    GOALS OF A CYBERSECURITY FRAMEWORK... 20

    HOW TO SELECT A SUITABLE IT SECURITY FRAMEWORK.................................. 22

    EXAMPLES OF IT SECURITY STANDARDS AND FRAMEWORKS 23

    INTERNAL CONTROL GOALS 29

    INTERNAL CONTROL COMPONENTS 29

    DEVELOPING YOUR ORGANIZATION'S INTERNAL CONTROL SYSTEM 30

    UTILIZING THE COSO FRAMEWORK 31

    THE LIMITATIONS OF COSO FRAMEWORK 32

    SELECTING A SECURITY FRAMEWORK 33

CHAPTER THREE 34

CYBERSECURITY AWARENESS 34

    WHAT IS CYBERSECURITY AWARENESS? 34

    ESSENTIAL WAYS COMPANIES CAN RAISE EMPLOYEE AWARENESS OF CYBERSECURITY.. 35

    ADVANTAGES OF CYBER SECURITY AWARENESS ACROSS FIRMS AND ORGANIZATIONS 38

    BENEFITS OF CYBERSECURITY 39

    DISADVANTAGES OF CYBER SECURITY 41

    THE SIGNIFICANCE OF CYBER SECURITY IN OUR LIFE.. 43

    POSSIBLE CAREER OPTIONS IN CYBERSECURITY 46

    SECURITY SOFTWARE DEVELOPER 47

        HOW TO ADVANCE IN THIS CAREER 47

        WHAT IS A SECURITY SOFTWARE DEVELOPER?... 48

        SKILLS AND EXPERIENCE IN DEVELOPING SECURITY SOFTWARE 49

        WHAT DO SECURITY SOFTWARE DEVELOPERS DO?.. 50

        SECURITY SOFTWARE DEVELOPER JOB DESCRIPTION 51

    SECURITY ARCHITECT 52

        STEPS TO FOLLOW WHEN PURSUING A CAREER AS A SECURITY ARCHITECT. 53

- *WHAT IS A SECURITY ARCHITECT?* 55
  - SECURITY ARCHITECT SKILLS 56
  - WHAT DO SECURITY ARCHITECTS DO? 57
  - SECURITY ARCHITECT JOB DESCRIPTION 57
- *SECURITY CONSULTANT* 58
  - PREPARING FOR A CAREER AS A SECURITY CONSULTANT 59
- *WHAT IS A SECURITY CONSULTANT?* 60
  - SECURITY CONSULTANT SKILLS AND EXPERIENCE 61
  - WHAT DO SECURITY CONSULTANTS DO? 62
  - SECURITY CONSULTANT JOB DESCRIPTION 64
- *INFORMATION SECURITY ANALYST* 66
  - FOUR STEPS TO BECOMING A SECURITY ANALYST 67
- *WHAT IS A SECURITY ANALYST?* 69
  - SECURITY ANALYST SKILLS AND EXPERIENCE 69
  - WHAT DO SECURITY ANALYSTS DO? 71
  - SECURITY ANALYST JOB DESCRIPTION 71
- *ETHICAL HACKERS* 72
  - ROLE OF AN ETHICAL HACKER 74
  - THE SKILLS REQUIRED TO BECOME AN ETHICAL HACKER 76
  - ETHICAL HACKER CERTIFICATIONS AND EDUCATION 78
  - HOW TO GET EXPERIENCE AS AN ETHICAL HACKER 80
  - TYPICAL ETHICAL HACKING ASSIGNMENTS 81
  - Threat modeling 81
  - Security assessment 82
  - Vulnerability threat assessment 83
  - Report writing 84
  - ETHICAL HACKING IN REVIEW 84
- *DIGITAL FORENSICS EXPERTS* 86
  - FOUR STEPS TO BECOMING A DIGITAL FORENSICS EXPERT 87
- *WHAT IS A DIGITAL FORENSICS?* 88
  - DIGITAL FORENSICS DEGREE, SKILLS, AND EXPERIENCE 89
  - WHAT DO DIGITAL FORENSICS EXPERTS DO? 91
  - DIGITAL FORENSICS EXPERT JOB DESCRIPTION 92
- *CHIEF INFORMATION SECURITY OFFICER* 93
  - FIVE STEPS TO BECOMING A CHIEF INFORMATION SECURITY OFFICER 93
- *WHAT IS A CHIEF INFORMATION SECURITY OFFICER?* 96

- CHIEF INFORMATION SECURITY OFFICERS' SKILLS AND EXPERIENCE 97
- WHAT DO CHIEF INFORMATION SECURITY OFFICERS DO? 98
- CHIEF INFORMATION SECURITY OFFICERS JOB DESCRIPTION 99

PENETRATION TESTER *100*
- SIX STEPS TO BECOMING A PENETRATION TESTER 101

WHAT IS A PENETRATION TESTER? *103*
- PENETRATION TESTER SKILLS AND EXPERIENCE 104
- WHAT DO PENETRATION TESTERS DO? 106
- PENETRATION TESTER JOB DESCRIPTION 107

CRYPTANALYST *109*

CRYPTANALYST VS. CRYPTOGRAPHER *110*
- FOUR STEPS TO BECOMING A CRYPTOANALYST 111

WHAT IS A CRYPTANALYST? *113*
- CRYPTANALYST SKILLS AND EXPERIENCE 114
- WHAT DO CRYPTANALYSTS DO? 115
- CRYPTANALYST JOB DESCRIPTION 116

SECURITY SYSTEMS ADMINISTRATOR *116*
- FIVE STEPS TO BECOMING A SECURITY ADMINISTRATOR 117
- WHAT IS A SECURITY ADMINISTRATOR? 119
- SECURITY ADMINISTRATOR SKILLS AND EXPERIENCE 119
- WHAT DO SECURITY ADMINISTRATORS DO? 120
- SECURITY ADMINISTRATOR JOB DESCRIPTION 121

HOW TO BEGIN A CAREER IN CYBERSECURITY *122*

DOMAINS OF CYBER SECURITY *126*

CHAPTER FOUR 129

CYBER SECURITY RISK ASSESSMENT 129
- *WHY PERFORM A CYBERSECURITY ASSESSMENT?* *130*
- *HOW DO YOU CONDUCT A CYBERSECURITY ASSESSMENT?* *132*
- *CYBER INCIDENT RESPONSE* *134*
- *STEPS TO RESPONDING TO CYBER INCIDENTS: A LIFECYCLE OF 6 PHASES* *134*
- *SECURITY EVENT TYPES AND RESPONSE STRATEGIES* *138*
- *HOW TO DETECT SECURITY INCIDENTS* *145*

CAUSES OF INCIDENT RESPONSE PROBLEMS 147

CASES OF SECURITY-RELATED OCCURRENCES 148

WHAT IS AN INCIDENT RESPONSE PLAN (IRP)? 149

REASONS WHY YOU NEED AN INCIDENT RESPONSE PLAN 150

    INCIDENT RESPONSE PLAN VS DISASTER RECOVERY PLAN 154

CHAPTER FIVE 155

CLOUD SECURITY ARCHITECTURE 155

WHAT IS CLOUD SECURITY ARCHITECTURE? 155

KEY ELEMENTS OF A CLOUD SECURITY ARCHITECTURE 156

SHARED RESPONSIBILITY WITHIN CLOUD SECURITY ARCHITECTURES 156

WHY IS CLOUD SECURITY ARCHITECTURE IMPORTANT? 158

CLOUD SECURITY ARCHITECTURES BY SERVICE MODEL 159

TYPES OF CLOUD SECURITY ARCHITECTURES 160

PRINCIPLES OF CLOUD SECURITY ARCHITECTURE 160

CLOUD SECURITY ARCHITECTURE THREATS 162

CHAPTER SIX 165

CYBERSECURITY ISSUES THAT ORGANIZATIONS FACE 165

SOCIAL ENGINEERING 166

RANSOMWARE 166

CLOUD COMPUTING ISSUES 167

DISTRIBUTED DENIAL-OF-SERVICE (DDOS) 167

ARTIFICIAL INTELLIGENCE (AI) AND MACHINE LEARNING (ML) 168

DATA BREACHES DUE TO REMOTE WORK 168

CRYPTO AND BLOCKCHAIN ATTACKS 169

THIRD-PARTY SOFTWARE 169

LACK OF INFORMATION SECURITY REPRESENTATION ON THE BOARD 170

CYBERSECURITY FOR SMALL BUSINESS 171

- *SMALL BUSINESSES ARE ATTRACTIVE TARGETS* *171*
- *HOW TO EVALUATE CYBER RISK* *173*
- *CYBER THREATS TO SMALL BUSINESSES* *174*
  - Malware threats 175
  - Email threats... 176
  - Video-teleconferencing threats 177
- *COMMON CYBER VULNERABILITIES*.. *178*
  - Behavioral vulnerabilities 178
  - Injection vulnerabilities 179
  - Sensitive data vulnerabilities... 179
  - Endpoint vulnerabilities... 180
  - Credential management vulnerabilities 181
- *CYBERSECURITY MITIGATION STRATEGIES* *182*
- *MITIGATING BEHAVIORAL VULNERABILITIES*... *182*
- *MITIGATING INJECTION ATTACKS* *183*
- *MITIGATING ATTACKS AGAINST SENSITIVE DATA*... *184*
- *MITIGATING ENDPOINT VULNERABILITIES* *185*
- *MITIGATING CREDENTIAL MANAGEMENT VULNERABILITIES*............................. *185*
- *CYBERSECURITY RESOURCES FOR SMALL BUSINESS* *186*

CHAPTER SEVEN 188

THE ROLE OF AI IN CYBER SECURITY 188

- *WHAT IS ARTIFICIAL INTELLIGENCE (AI)?* *188*
- *ARTIFICIAL INTELLIGENCE FOR CYBER SECURITY* *189*
- *WHAT IS THE ROLE OF ARTIFICIAL INTELLIGENCE IN CYBER SECURITY?* *189*
- *USE OF MACHINE LEARNING IN CYBERSPACE* *190*
- *CONUNDRUM OF AI AND CYBERSECURITY- POSSIBLE DRAWBACKS* *191*
- *HOW IS AI USED IN SECURITY?*... *192*
  - AUTOMATED MALWARE DETECTION AND PREVENTION 193
  - PHISHING AND SPAM DETECTION 194
  - FASTER AND ACCURATE ANOMALY DETECTION – SIEM AND SOAR PLATFORMS 195

SEARCHING FOR ZERO-DAY EXPLOITS 195
INCREASES THE SPEED OF DETECTION AND RESPONSE 196
DETECTION OF NEW THREATS 196
REDUCE THE NUMBER OF FALSE POSITIVES 197
DETECTING BOTS 198
PREDICTION OF BREACH RISK 198
SECURING AUTHENTICATION 198

CHAPTER EIGHT 200

THE VARIOUS TECHNIQUES USED BY HACKERS 200

CHAPTER NINE 208

POSSIBLE INDICATIONS YOU'RE SET UP FOR A CAREER IN CYBERSECURITY 208

PREREQUISITES FOR THINKING ABOUT A CAREER IN CYBER SECURITY 208

CYBERSECURITY CERTIFICATIONS 212

SECURING ENTRY-LEVEL CYBERSECURITY JOBS 214

A MANUAL ON CYBERSECURITY CODING 216

    Understanding Java 219
    C/C++ 220
    Python 221
    JavaScript? 222
    Understanding PHP 223
    Learning SQL 224
    Apple's Swift 225
    Learning Ruby 225
    Understanding Perl 226
    Lisp 227

PROGRAMMING FOR CYBERSECURITY IN CONCLUSION 227

INDEX 231

CHAPTER ONE

INTRODUCTION TO CYBERSECURITY

The worst cybersecurity error a modern organization can make is to think "it probably won't affect us." The threat to cybersecurity is real, and it is currently a problem on a worldwide scale. In the current digital era, everyone and every organization faces the possibility of a system hack, ransomware attack, data leak, or infection, regardless of their size or industry. The attackers of today are not like the lone hackers of yesterday. They run organized crime networks and frequently act like start-up companies, hiring highly qualified programmers to create brand-new online attacks.

Due to the growing amount of sensitive data that businesses of all sizes must secure, cybersecurity is becoming increasingly important. As the scale and scope of risks continue to expand swiftly, new opportunities are opening up for experienced data professionals in a range of industries.

The practice of protecting network systems, computers, servers, mobile devices, electronic devices, and data from malicious attack is known as cybersecurity. It is often referred to as information technology security or electronic information security. According to experts, the rise of IoT-connected devices, cloud-based apps, a range of technology initiatives, and strict privacy protection rules are driving the market for cyber security to grow swiftly. Security is without a doubt one of the sectors with the fastest growth. But there is a serious shortage of experienced personnel.

Before you go into some of the security's complexities, you need have a clear understanding of the fundamental security objectives. Some fundamental ideas are part of an organization's core security goals. These principles serve as the foundation for many security-related choices at many levels. These foundational concepts should be thoroughly understood in order to provide a solid security base.

As more digital information is gathered and shared, its security is becoming progressively more crucial for the safety and economic stability of our nation. At the corporate level, everyone is responsible for protecting the brand, information, and clients of the business. At the state level, there is a threat to both national security and the safety and well-being of the population.

Governments keep a ton of records and personal data about their citizens, along with private government information that is routinely targeted by hackers. The only way to boost public confidence in government services is through education and information. For cybersecurity, education is a necessity. Then, let's examine what cybersecurity comprises.

WHAT IS CYBERSECURITY?

The term "cybersecurity" refers to a group of policies, tools, and methods used to prevent damaging intrusions that might give illegal access to servers, computers, networks, electronic systems, data, and mobile devices. A different definition of cybersecurity is the process of protecting important systems and sensitive data against online threats.

Cybersecurity measures, often known as IT security, are designed to thwart assaults on networked systems and applications, whether those threats originate from within or outside of a business.

A wide range of security measures are referred to as cybersecurity. Typical cybersecurity categories include:

- **Application Security**: Applications that have been compromised may make it simpler for unauthorized individuals to access data. Application security defends against cyberattacks on hardware, software, and applications alike.
- **Operational security**: Contains all aspects, including access rights and decisions and practices that determine where and how data will be shared or stored. It highlights the need of safeguarding data assets.
- **Information security**: is interested in protecting data's integrity and privacy while it is being stored and transported.
- **Network security**: Network security is a method of defending computer networks against opportunistic viruses or deliberate attackers.
- **Database and Infrastructure security**: Physical barriers are the focus of this area of cybersecurity. These measures are used to deter burglars from entering hardware or stealing it. This may be anything as straightforward as a lock or as complex as a sophisticated security system.
- **Mobile security**: Every day, more private data is uploaded to mobile devices. Therefore, all phones must

be adequately shielded. Strong password usage, ensuring that no information is stored on a phone unless it is required, and providing instructions on how to access mobile services safely are all important components of mobile security.
- **End-user Education**: This subcategory of cybersecurity deals with people, a highly unpredictable component. End-user education aims to educate users about potential risks to their online safety as well as the best security measures to adopt.
- **Cloud security**: The entire cloud is now a part of using the internet. Employees can upload information to the cloud, where it can be retrieved without starting a long email chain. However, a company's susceptibility is also increased by the cloud. The safety of the data stored in the cloud is the basic objective of cloud security.

WHAT'S CYBERCRIME?

Cybercrime is any criminal activity that involves or is directed towards a computer, a computer network, or a networked device. Most cybercrime is committed by hackers or cybercriminals who are wanting money, though this is not always the case. Both people and groups can commit cybercrime.

Some cybercriminals are well-organized, use cutting-edge techniques, and possess advanced technical abilities. There are some amateur hackers. Rarely does computer damage in cyberspace aim to achieve anything but advance financial interests? These could be political or personal.

Any behavior that fundamentally violates human sensibilities may fall under the category of cybercrime. Cybercrime is more accurately defined as the use of computer technology to commit a crime; this includes any actions that endanger a society's ability to maintain appropriate balance. Therefore, both established and newly emergent cybercrimes are covered by this concept.

To address this problem, the following topic can be used to group and study cybercrime:

1) Individual

2) Property

3) Government

4) Society

CYBERCRIME AGAINST INDIVIDUAL

Cybercriminals have victimized people. This kind of offense had a big effect on the offender's personality. The user is vulnerable to the following forms of cybercrimes:

- **Cyber-stalking:** Whether stalking is carried out through a computer or email, the term "cyber-stalking" refers to the following someone to harass or disgrace them online. Frequently, it is done by engaging in unlawful activities like identity theft, extortion, defamation, spoofing, etc. Someone may create fictional websites, forums, and spam messages with threats, false profiles, or abusive emails in order to cyberstalk.

- **Cyber-Defamation:** for online dissemination of misleading information. What is said and written words, signs, or other visual cues may cause harm. The individual who made the false statement must have intended to damage the accuser's reputation in the eyes of the general public. When someone posts a false statement online using a social networking site, email, or other kind of cyber-technology, this is known as cyber-defamation.

- **Cracking:** when a user accesses a computer system without my knowledge or consent and tampers with private information.

- **E-mail harassment:** involves the dissemination of letters, links, and file attachments and is a frequent form of harassment. As more individuals use social media sites like Twitter, Facebook, Instagram, etc., harassment is becoming more common.

- **Phishing:** In order to get sensitive personal information, a criminal may send an email asking the receiver to update his records or, in some situations, validate the information on his credit card. This practice is known as phishing.

- **Hacking:** Hacking, to put it simply, is the act of breaking into a computer without permission. It's not necessarily against the law to hack into systems since "ethical hacking" enables hackers to gain lawful access to computer networks. But hacking becomes illegal behavior when a hacker gains access to someone's computer network without that person's knowledge or permission.

- **E-mail spoofing:** In this instance, an attacker uses their victim's cell phone number to send emails and SMS messages while assuming their victim's identity. It is a highly lethal cybercrime committed against any individual.

- **Carding:** This phrase describes the practice of criminals taking money out of the victim's bank account using false credit and debit cards for their own financial gain. This subset of cybercrimes frequently involves the misuse of ATM cards.

- **Child pornography:** The perpetrators of this cybercrime create or spread materials that profit from the sexual exploitation of youngsters. In India, this is regarded as one of the worst types of cybercrime.

CYBERCRIME AGAINST THE PROPERTY

The second category of cybercrimes includes crimes committed against property, such as computer trespassing, the distribution of damaging malware, computer vandalism, and unlawful possession of digital data.

- **Cybersquatting:** When two people contend to have registered the same domain name first and to have the exclusive right to use it before the other, or when they use a phrase that is similar, this occurs.
- **Intellectual property:** When an owner's rights are forcibly removed in whole or in part, crimes are

committed. Copyright infringement, software piracy, patent, trademark, service mark, and design infringement, as well as computer source code theft, are the most frequent IPR breaches.
- **Hacking Computer Systems**: Hackers prey on well-known websites like Facebook, Twitter, Instagram, and blogging platforms through illegal computer access or control. These attacks weren't carried out solely for monetary gain or to damage the reputation of a certain individual or business. In April 2013, MMM India was hacked.
- **Transmitting Viruses:** In order to alter or destroy a computer or file, a virus attaches to it first before moving on to other computers or data on a network. Cyber trespassing is the illegal act of accessing a computer or network without the owner's consent and changing, misusing, disrupting, or destroying data.
- **Cyber Vandalism:** Information or data kept on a computer may be damaged or lost when network service is halted or interrupted. The deliberate destruction of another person's property is known as vandalism. Any computer component theft could result from these actions.

CRIME AGAINST GOVERNMENT

The third category of cybercrime is crime against government. Although it belongs to this category, cybercrime is a unique kind of crime. The expansion of the internet has shown how individuals and groups may use cyberspace to undermine national governments and pose a threat to the residents of other countries. Such acts take the form of terrorism when a person "cracks" into a website run by a government or the military.

- **Cyberterrorism-** is perilous on both a national and worldwide scale. Terrorists have targeted critical computer networks, sent hate mail and created websites, among other things, in their attacks on the Internet. The security and honor of the nation are threatened by cyberterrorism tactics.
- **Distribution of Printed Software** – This refers to the act of moving "Printed Software" (official documents and government data) from one device to another. Possession of illegal information - Terrorists can easily use the Internet to access any material and store it for use in furthering their ideological, political, financial, or religious objectives.
- **Cyberwarfare -** This phrase refers to hacking for political purposes, such as sabotage and espionage. This type of information warfare is usually contrasted with conventional warfare, although both its political overtones and its authenticity make this comparison questionable.

CYBERCRIME AGAINST THE SOCIETY

The fourth level of crime classification is this. if a crime is done with the intent to use cyber techniques to hurt a sizable population or society at large.

- **Child pornography**: This is the act of producing, gaining access to, or transmitting materials that profit from child sexual abuse.
- **Financial Crimes**: Attacks on phone networking and network sites using phony emails or messages sent over the internet, such as the use of credit cards and the illegal acquisition of passwords.
- **Falsification:** This refers to deceiving a substantial number of individuals by sending threatening emails, which is now a normal requirement for daily living since online business payments have become commonplace.

TYPES OF CYBERCRIME

Here are some specific examples of the many different types of cybercrime:

- Email and online fraud.
- Identity theft, in which private information is obtained and used.
- Theft of banking or credit card data.
- Business-related data theft and sales.
- Making a money demand using cyber extortion to halt a threatened attack.
- Ransomware attacks are one type of internet extortion.
- Crypto-jacking, which is the practice of hackers mining bitcoins using resources that they do not own.
- Cyber invasions, in which cybercriminals gain access to government or commercial entities' data.

WHO ARE CYBERCRIMINALS?

Cybercriminals are individuals or groups who use technology to commit evil deeds on digital networks or systems in order to steal private customer or employee information and earn money.

While cybercriminals hack and access computer systems with malicious intentions, hackers only look for new and inventive ways to use a system, whether for good or bad. They typically carry out operations on big victim populations that are only comparable in terms of the platforms they use, how they behave online, or the apps they use.

The laws governing cybercrime are continually changing in many countries throughout the world. Law enforcement agencies continue to have trouble locating, seizing, proving, and convicting cybercriminals.

Not all hackers are also cybercriminals because hacking is not always seen as a criminality.

MOTIVATION FOR CYBERCRIMINALS

The reasons behind cybercriminals' actions can be rather simple. The great bulk of things are made up of money and information. According to a Verizon Enterprise research, 93% of the motives behind assaults are financial and espionage-related. The less typical but more diverse mix of incentives is also frequently referred to as "FIG" (Fun, Ideology, and Grudges).Depending on the target, whether the attacks are being carried out on the cybercriminal's initiative or under contract, and who stands to profit monetarily from a successful cybercrime, the key objectives can alter. This kind is demonstrated by the following:

Money

This could be the reason behind many other attack types, including ransomware, phishing, and data theft (for sale or ransom of records). A cryptocurrency is commonly utilized for smaller transactions; otherwise, wire transfers are used for larger transactions. The victim will either be directly used by the cybercriminal for financial benefit or they will profit from the selling of their data on underground markets. Hackers, like everyone else motivated by money, want the most payback for the amount of work they put in. A hacker can easily conduct a successful attack by focusing on small businesses or industries with lax security rules.

Competition

Breaking into a manufacturer's system can be advantageous whether it's for intellectual property (IP), extortion, competitive intelligence, sabotage (creating a PR nightmare), or other reasons. This is particularly dangerous given the (lack of) technical sophistication of systems in every industry sector with sophisticated property rights at its core, whether it be in technology, pharmaceuticals, high-tech manufacturing, resource exploitation, general utilities, industrial systems, or related fields.

Political Purpose

As we can see with numerous state actors, more and more people are turning to cybercrime as a means to achieve their political goals. Even if they are not direct targets, state action is becoming a worry for all businesses, whether they use hacking to influence elections, cut off a country's power supply, or spread ransomware.

FIGs (Fun, Ideology, Grudge)

Some crooks like exposing weaknesses in their victims. Some people might just never forgive, whether it's because of subpar customer service, a terrible product, or to settle a personal score. Others do it to advance the disclosure of information they think is in the public's interest or for ideological reasons.

They may utilize one of the aforementioned tactics, or they may launch DDoS attacks to achieve their goals, albeit that tactic may also be employed for political or competitive purposes.

Others

This category includes any other ad hoc reasons for data breaches. System flaws and employee errors fall under this category.

Similar to the Fun category, some breaches have no malicious intent. However, a breach is still a breach, and the results might be dire, regardless of the motivation.

THE KEY CONCEPT OF CYBER SECURITY

Despite the broad definition of "cyber security" it is based on "The CIA Triad" a set of three fundamental ideas.

It is composed of transparency, honesty, and confidentiality. This model is meant to guide the organization with regard to information security policy on cyber security.

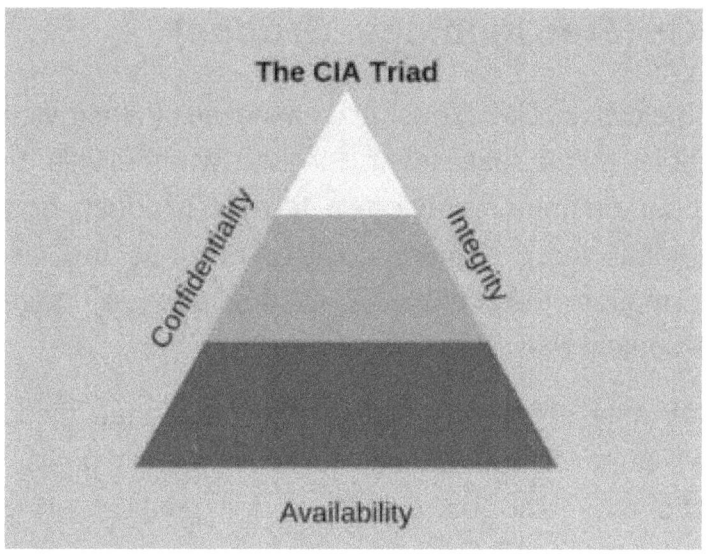

Confidentiality

It defines the rules that limit access to information. Confidentiality is the practice of adopting measures to thwart online criminals and hackers from obtaining private data.

By approving the suitable individuals in a department, information is made available to or withheld from people in an organization based on its category. They are adequately instructed on how to share information and safeguard their accounts with strong passwords as well.

They can change how data is handled within an organization to ensure data protection. Numerous measures, including as two-factor authentication, data encryption, data classification, biometric verification, and security tokens, can be taken to safeguard the confidentiality of information.

Integrity

This guarantees the consistency, accuracy, and dependability of the data across time. This means that the data shouldn't be added to, deleted from, or have any illegal access while it's being transported.

There are some things that should be done to ensure an organization's safety. User access control and file permissions are the safeguards that prevent data compromise. Technologies and techniques must also be used to detect any changes or security breaches in the data. Many organizations use checksums, especially cryptographic checksums, to verify the accuracy of data.

To handle data loss, unintended deletion, and even cyberattacks, regular backups should be available. Cloud backups are currently the most dependable solution for this.

Availability

It is crucial to keep all necessary components, including as hardware, software, networks, devices, and security equipment, up to date and ensure availability. This will provide continual access to and proper functioning of the data while providing enough bandwidth to permit ongoing communication between the components.

In addition, extra security measures must be made in case of disaster or traffic congestion. Use tools like firewalls, backup solutions, disaster recovery plans, and proxy servers to defend against DoS attacks.

A solid cybersecurity plan must navigate across several security layers, particularly when it comes to computers, hardware, networks, software, and shared data.

CONCEPT OF CYBERSPACE

A quick-connecting, non-geographical global community can be thought of as cyberspace. Cyberspace is an interactive system of computer networks where individuals may connect online and do a variety of things, including conduct business, share knowledge, assist one another, create artistic media, take action, and have political conversations. Online is the current frontier and the common heritage of humanity, but tragically some people abuse it, turning cyberspace into a new frontier with new kinds of crime.

William Gibson initially used the term "cyberspace" which he later described as "an evocative and meaningless" buzzword that could be used as a code for all of his concepts of cybernetic (transforming a text to hide its meaning). Today, it is employed to explain anything relating to computers, IT, and the internet, and the intricate online culture. The term "Cyber

Space" also refers to the digital environment in which all information technology-based interactions and transactions occur. Cyberspace cannot be positioned in space. It is made up of immaterial elements including personal information, email addresses, websites, forums, and social media profiles.

THREATS AND ATTACKS IN CYBERSECURITY

To prevent a cyber threat or assault, it is essential to understand what they are. The National Institute of Standards and Technology, or NIST, routinely covers the major categories of cyber risks and cyberattacks, which everyone should be aware of. They include:

CYBER THREATS

Criminals may use a variety of techniques to try to break into a company network and compromise important information. If staff members are aware of how these attacks are carried out, they might be halted in their tracks. Some of the most common hazards in the world of cybersecurity include:

- **Trojans:** Trojan horse exploits are an everyday threat to cybersecurity. A hacker attempts to send a file containing a virus to a company or a person in this type of attack by disguising it as a legitimate file. When the file is opened, the virus is released, and the attack begins.
- **Hacking:** Hacking is without a doubt the most common type of cybersecurity threat. The goal of hacking is to gain permission to use the company's system. On

occasion, information has been stolen by hackers. In other circumstances, hackers can try to launch a brute-force attack, in which they merely try every combination quickly until the network is unlocked.

- **Spear phishing:** Spear phishing is a variation on the standard fishing technique. In contrast to phishing attempts, which often target numerous people at once, spear-phishing assaults frequently leverage profiles on social media and other intelligence to personally target a single person. When the victim provides their account information, the hacker can then access the network.
- **Phishing:** Phishing attacks are a frequent type of cybersecurity risk. In an attempt to get someone to divulge their login information, a hacker may pose as a member of the company's staff. Using these credentials, the hacker can then start an attack on the company's database.
- **Malware:** Malware is a general phrase that covers a wide range of infections and cybersecurity risks. Malware can cause a number of grave issues. For instance, certain viruses merely cause the internet to lag, making it difficult for the network to function. In other cases, malware might attempt to obtain private information before making it available to the general public. Malware identification can be aided by powerful security solutions, which is crucial.
- **Social Engineering:** Simply put, spear phishing attempts are also known as "social engineering" attacks. These assaults fall under the category of social engineering since they use human interaction to

persuade victims to divulge their login and password. The best way to prevent these assaults is to educate the staff about how they happen, the risks they pose, and what to do if they think they are the target of one.
- **Cross-site Scripting:** commonly shortened to XSS. This is a common weakness that hackers may exploit in specific scripts. Web applications insert client-side scripting into well-known websites. Using these scripts, hackers can gain access to private information when visitors visit the website.
- **DNS Spoofing:** This attack is frequently referred to as "DNS cache poisoning". During this attack, a flawed data code is introduced into the resolver of the DNS system. When a server is accessed by this malicious code, the server eventually produces misleading data. As a result, hackers have access to the company's confidential information.
- **Ransomware:** One of the deadliest types of cyberattacks out there, ransomware assaults can completely shut down a company's network or server. During a ransomware attack, the entire system is encrypted, making it worthless. Business networks will then be held captive by the hackers until a ransom is paid by the company. Businesses can try to unlock the network on their own, but it will cost them money and time to do so. If an attack is launched against a healthcare system, it may even be able to shut down essential life support systems.

CHAPTER TWO

CYBERSECURITY FRAMEWORK

An IT security framework is a collection of defined procedures that controls the deployment and ongoing management of information security solutions. These frameworks provide as a roadmap for reducing vulnerabilities and managing risk.

Information security professionals specify and prioritize the tasks required to manage enterprise security using frameworks. Frameworks are often used to prepare for compliance and other IT audits. The framework must therefore be able to support the precise specifications listed in the standard or rule.

Organizations may create frameworks to handle specific information security challenges, such as industry-specific requirements or varied regulatory compliance objectives. Frameworks come in a variety of sizes and degrees of complexity. Given that today's frameworks frequently overlap, it is imperative to pick one that successfully fulfills operational, compliance, and audit requirements.

GOALS OF A CYBERSECURITY FRAMEWORK

The primary goal of the majority of cybersecurity frameworks is to increase the industry's ability to withstand cyberattacks. They achieve this by using the framework's suggestions to help even the tiniest businesses put effective security measures in place. The professionals involved in creating these standards are typically out of reach for smaller enterprises, but the framework allows everyone to benefit from their knowledge.

Regulation compliance for these firms might also be aided by cybersecurity frameworks. As a direct result of the increasing frequency of data breaches involving both corporate and personal data, numerous regulatory bodies from various industries have developed information security standards that businesses operating within their purview are obligated to abide by. These laws almost always reference cybersecurity frameworks, even if they may vary depending on the firm.

When creating policies, standards, and operational duties for information security management, frameworks provide a place to start.

Because security requirements frequently overlap, there are numerous "crosswalks" that can be used to demonstrate compliance with various regulatory standards. In Section 5 of ISO 27002, the "Align, Plan, and Organize" section of COBIT, and the "Internal Environment" section of the Committee of Sponsoring Organizations of the Treadway Commission (COSO) framework, for example, information security policy is described. It is described as "Assigned Security Responsibility" under HIPAA in the "Maintain an Information Security Policy" section of the PCI DSS.

Using a common framework like ISO 27002, a firm can produce crosswalks to demonstrate compliance with multiple legislation, including HIPAA, Sarbanes-Oxley, PCI DSS, and Graham-Leach-Bliley.

HOW TO SELECT A SUITABLE IT SECURITY FRAMEWORK

There are several reasons why one particular IT security architecture might be used. Regulatory requirements or the type of industry could be decisive factors. Publicly traded companies, for example, might decide to use COBIT to comply with Sarbanes-Oxley, whereas the healthcare sector might wish to consider HITRUST. The ISO 27000 Series of information security frameworks, on the other hand, applies to both the public and private sectors.

Although putting ISO standards into practice might be time-consuming, they are helpful when a business seeks ISO 27000 certification to demonstrate its information security capabilities. NIST Special Publication (SP) 800-53 is the standard that U.S. federal agencies use, but any business can use it to develop a technology-specific information security plan.

Using these frameworks, security professionals can create and manage an information security program. The only horrible choice among these frames is to make no decision at all.

EXAMPLES OF IT SECURITY STANDARDS AND FRAMEWORKS

1. ISO 27000 Series

The ISO 27000 Series was developed by IOS, the International Organization for Standardization. It is a flexible information security architecture that can be applied by organizations of all sizes.

The criteria and procedures for creating an information security management system are laid out in the two primary standards, ISO 27002 and 27001 (ISMS). Having an ISMS is a crucial audit and compliance activity. ISO 27000, which also provides an overview and vocabulary, defines the requirements for the ISMS program. In ISO 27002, a code of conduct for developing ISMS controls is described.

Through audit and certification processes, which are often provided by independent businesses recognized by ISO and other regulatory organizations, the ISO 27000 Series standards are validated.

The ISO 27000 Series has 60 standards that address various information security issues, such as:

- The acquisition and protection of digital evidence are defined by ISO 27037.
- The standard ISO 27040 defines storage security.
- ISO 27031 offers instructions on IT disaster recovery plans and related tasks.
- Cloud computing is designated by ISO 27018.

- ISO 27799 is helpful for firms that must adhere to HIPAA regulations that information security in healthcare is defined.

2. NIST SP 800-53

NIST has developed a substantial number of IT standards, many of which are concerned with information security. Nearly every aspect of information security is covered by the NIST SP 800 Series, which was initially published in 1990 and has an increasing emphasis on cloud security.

NIST SP 800-53 is the information security standard used by U.S. government organizations; it is also often used in the private sector. The application of SP 800-53 has helped the NIST Cybersecurity Framework and other information security frameworks (CSF).

3. NIST SP 800-171

NIST SP 800-171 has become more well-known as a result of the US Department of Defense's requirements for contractor adherence to security frameworks. Government contractors frequently become the target of cyberattacks because of their proximity to federal information networks. Government vendors and subcontractors require an IT security framework in order to compete for federal and state procurement opportunities.

The controls included in the NIST SP 800-171 framework are closely similar to NIST SP 800-53, although being less specific and more general. A crosswalk between the two standards can be made using NIST SP 800-171 as the basis in case a business has to prove compliance with NIST SP 800-53. Since they can employ the additional controls in NIST SP 800-53 to show compliance as they grow, smaller businesses now have more latitude.

4. NIST CSF

NIST was instructed to develop the NIST Framework for Improving Critical Infrastructure Cybersecurity, or NIST CSF, by Executive Order 13636, which was released in February 2013. It was developed to address issues with transportation, communications, energy and water production, and other critical components of the American infrastructure. These industries must all maintain a high degree of readiness since nation-state actors have all targeted them because of their importance.

In contrast to previous NIST frameworks, the NIST CSF is focused on risk analysis and risk management. The five risk management phases of identification, protection, detection, reaction, and recovery form the foundation for the security solutions in the framework. Like any IT security projects, these phases require support from senior management. NIST CSF is available to the public and business sectors.

5. NIST SP 1800 Series

The NIST SP 1800 Series of manuals is a complement to the NIST SP 800 Series of standards and frameworks. The books in the SP 1800 Series provide instructions on how to apply standards-based cybersecurity solutions in real-world circumstances.

The following is provided by the SP 1800 Series publications: examples of specific situations and capabilities;

- detailed instructions that use a variety of goods and are based on experience to produce the desired outcome;
- modular advice on putting capabilities into practice for enterprises of all sizes;
- Component specifications, installation, configuration, and integration details so that companies may readily replicate the process for themselves.

6. COBIT

Middle of the 1990s saw the creation of COBIT by the non-profit ISACA organization of IT governance specialists. ISACA provides the prestigious Certified Information Systems Auditor and Certified Information Security Manager certificates.

COBIT's original objective was to reduce IT risks. New business and technology advancements are included in COBIT 5, which was released in 2012 and helps businesses balance IT and business goals. The most recent version is COBIT 2019. This is the Sarbanes-Oxley compliance framework that is most widely used. Numerous books and professional certifications cover the COBIT requirements.

7. CIS Controls

The Center for Internet Security (CIS) Critical Security Controls, Version 8 includes technical security and operational controls that can be applied in any situation (formerly the SANS Top 20). Instead of addressing risk analysis or risk management like NIST CSF, it is solely focused on reducing risk and increasing resilience for technological infrastructures.

Controls include the following:

- Inventory and Control of Enterprise Assets
- Data Protection
- Audit Log Management
- Malware Defenses
- Penetration Testing

CIS Controls interface with current risk management systems to aid in addressing identified hazards. They are important resources for IT departments that lack a technical foundation in information security.

8. HITRUST Common Security Framework

The HITRUST Common Security Framework also includes criteria for risk analysis and risk management in addition to operational requirements. The framework, which contains 14 distinct control types, can be applied by healthcare organizations in almost any form of organization.

Because HITRUST places such a high value on documentation and procedures, every business must make a substantial effort to comply. As a result, many companies realize that they need to focus their HITRUST initiatives. The level of effort required to apply this framework increases due to the cost of HITRUST certification and its upkeep. The third-party assessment of the certification adds another level of authenticity.

9. GDPR

Global businesses must adhere to the GDPR framework of security criteria in order to protect the security and privacy of the personal information of EU citizens. The GDPR mandates protections for preventing unauthorized access to stored data as well as access control techniques like least privilege, role-based access, and multifactor authentication.

10. COSO

COSO is an initiative created in cooperation by five professional associations. Risk management is covered by its 2017 framework, while internal controls are addressed by its 2013 framework. The COSO framework's initial iteration was developed in 1992, and the most recent version was released in 2013. To understand the framework, you must first understand what it covers. Internal control in accordance with COSO:

- Focuses on attaining objectives in reporting, compliance, or operations.
- Is a never-ending process.
- Is not solely dependent on written policies and processes, but also on actual human conduct.
- Provides top management with a sufficient level of security assurance.
- Can be adjusted to suit the needs of any department, unit, or procedure as well as those of the entire organization.

INTERNAL CONTROL GOALS

The COSO framework divides internal control objectives into three categories: operations, reporting, and compliance.

Operations: The major focus of goals like performance goals and safeguarding the business's assets against fraud is the efficacy and efficiency of your business operations.

Reporting: The organization's reporting practices, including internal and external financial reporting as well as non-financial reporting, are to be open, prompt, and reliable.

Compliance: The organization's internal control objectives are focused on adhering to the necessary rules and regulations.

INTERNAL CONTROL COMPONENTS

According to the COSO architecture, an internal control system has five parts. The control environment is defined as the "collection of standards, processes, and structures that serve as the foundation for applying internal controls throughout the firm." Your involvement in this entails:

- Ethical principles
- A dedication to hiring professionals
- Guidelines for human resources
- Organizational layout
- Guidelines for human resources

Your firm must take into account all areas of risk assessment, including the process for assessing risks against risk tolerances and the capacity to create goals and analyze their viability for your business.

Control activities: Internal control objectives can be achieved by implementing the "control activities" (described by organizational policies and procedures). These include, among other things, "authorizations and approvals, verifications, reconciliations, and business performance reviews."

The **information** and **communication** component recognizes these two elements as essential to any internal control system. The importance of pertinent, trustworthy information for operations control is stressed by COSO. A strong system depends on both clear expectations being conveyed to outside parties and on internal communications that emphasize the importance of control responsibilities.

Not least of all, keeping internal controls in place is just as important as creating them. Use continuous assessments that are part of your business operations as well as regular, independent evaluations that are tailored to your level of risk, the effectiveness of your system, and the requirements of any legislation that may be in force.

DEVELOPING YOUR ORGANIZATION'S INTERNAL CONTROL SYSTEM

According to the COSO framework, an effective internal control system reduces the risk of failing to achieve objectives to a manageable level. Be sure of the following things when developing your system:

- The five components work together to form a cohesive system.
- All five components are present and working properly.
- It enables the company to foresee external issues that may hinder your ability to accomplish your goals and make the required preparations for them.
- It complies with reporting laws, rules, and guidelines.
- It complies with all relevant laws and regulations etc.

Although COSO admits that its architecture ought to help you develop an internal control system that prevents fraud, it has a number of drawbacks. For instance, no technology, no matter how good, can protect you from human error, bad decisions, and inescapable external factors.

UTILIZING THE COSO FRAMEWORK

After reading the COSO framework, senior management and key decision-makers in your firm should assess your current internal control system utilizing it. Does your system adhere to the necessary standards for efficiency? If not, create strategies to enhance it using the COSO model.

Additionally, it is important to familiarize lower-level managers and employees with the COSO framework. Using the information, make suggestions to higher management. Form a group of staffers from various levels to come up with ideas for a better internal control system.

Additionally, every employee needs to take their obligation to stop fraud seriously. Adhere to workplace policies that support the COSO framework. As an illustration, always submit accurate, timely reports and strictly abide by anti-fraud standards.

THE LIMITATIONS OF COSO FRAMEWORK

The COSO framework can be used to create or modify an internal control system. But there are a few limitations.

For instance, the framework is purposely wide in order to be applicable to a range of industries and procedures. According to experts from East Carolina University, "more intricate organizations" (i.e. those with a range of processes and complex data systems) can experience problems with this functionality.

They also state that "the ability to establish a strong, formal control environment is a precondition for the proper execution of the COSO framework, despite the framework providing limited implementation aid" Small businesses and startups could feel powerless and overburdened, which leads them to select a model with a more solid base.

Additionally, the COSO framework is ineffectively supportive of dealing with objectives that fall under multiple categories. The categories of operating, reporting, and compliance responsibilities are not always clearly separable.

If you're looking to create or improve an internal control system, the COSO framework is a suitable option.

SELECTING A SECURITY FRAMEWORK

In light of the rise in cyberattacks and data breaches, organizations need to have a strong cybersecurity architecture. To lower their cyber risk, organizations should follow the best practices recommended in cybersecurity frameworks. Businesses can utilize a wide range of cybersecurity frameworks. This is why choosing the best framework for your business may be difficult. Additionally, a variety of industry and regulatory needs mandate that several cybersecurity frameworks be cross-referenced. Understanding the similarities and differences between the main security frameworks will help you create a cybersecurity compliance program for your company that is more successful.

It's important to consider your sector and any applicable regulatory requirements before choosing a cybersecurity reference framework. If this applies to you, the appropriate framework must be used. However, I suggest that the vast majority of businesses use the NIST Cyber Security Framework (CSF). It is comprehensive, simple to understand, and tightly aligned with other standards and compliance requirements. The 5-area concept makes perfect sense:

- .Determine what demands protection (**Identify**)
- Take necessary precautions (**Protect**)
- Monitor and become ready (**Detect**)
- Control security occurrences (**Respond**)
- Knowing what to do in case something goes wrong. (**Recover**)

CHAPTER THREE

CYBERSECURITY AWARENESS

In our mobile, connected culture, cybersecurity awareness is more crucial than ever because the human element provides one of the biggest cybersecurity threats. If you ask any IT security professional, they will all give you the same answer.

According to the 2014 Cyber Security Intelligence Index, a stunning 95% of all security concerns are caused by human mistake. The most prevalent mistake is double-clicking on an unsafe URL or an infected attachment. Other common errors include failing to patch systems, employing weak passwords and default user names, misplacing laptops and mobile devices, and using the incorrect email address to unintentionally reveal confidential information.

WHAT IS CYBERSECURITY AWARENESS?

It transcends knowledge, Action is not knowledge. Security awareness is the combination of knowledge with attitudes and behaviors that protect our information assets. Understanding cybersecurity entails being aware of the risks and taking the appropriate measures to mitigate them.

Employee knowledge is one of the elements that companies occasionally overlook when developing a cybersecurity plan. If employees have the tools and knowledge to recognize warning signs of a security issue before they arise, they can prevent a potential data breach that might seriously impact a company's operations, finances, and reputation.

ESSENTIAL WAYS COMPANIES CAN RAISE EMPLOYEE AWARENESS OF CYBERSECURITY

1. Include cybersecurity in the onboarding process.

A quick way to persuade employees that cybersecurity is a key issue is to include it in the onboarding process. By instructing personnel on their responsibilities for preserving information security, businesses may build a solid defense against cyber threats. But it's important to keep in mind that cybersecurity education shouldn't end with onboarding; rather, ongoing cybersecurity marketing needs to be included in your company's strategy to increase awareness, which brings us to the following problem.

2. Regularly train your cybersecurity team

Every employee, regardless of position, needs to be made aware of the most recent cyber threats and educated how to recognize and avoid them. Maintaining cybersecurity isn't just the responsibility of the IT department. Every effective cybersecurity plan requires personnel who have undergone the necessary training. Through a thorough security awareness training program that will improve everyone's understanding of cybersecurity, employees will have the assurance and knowledge required to recognize cyber threats, effectively respond to them in order to prevent them, as well as the process of escalation.

However, it's imperative to guarantee that cybersecurity training is regularly conducted, not just once. By doing this, a culture of security awareness is created, and the importance of cybersecurity is emphasized. Employee training can dramatically improve your defenses because they are your company's first line of protection against cyber-attacks.

3. Use cybersecurity exercises

Using a cyber drill, which focuses on assessing employee reaction times in a simulated environment, is a great way to evaluate an organization's security. Cyber exercises simulate cyberattacks and evaluate a business' security procedures. They are frequently carried out by an internal or outside team. Different drills assess the talents of various staff groups. By replicating a phishing attack, for instance, a phishing simulation evaluates employees' alertness when it comes to recognizing and avoiding phishing frauds.

Based on how many employees fell for the simulated phishing assault, a corporation can determine whether to concentrate more of its efforts on promoting awareness of other areas of cybersecurity or on phishing during the following cybersecurity training awareness session.

4. Establish reliable cybersecurity policies and practices

A great way to increase cybersecurity awareness is to make sure that sound cybersecurity rules and procedures are in place. An organization's information security obligations for each employee are spelled out in a written cybersecurity policy. The accepted standards of behavior for actions like utilizing social media, delivering sensitive information via email in a proper manner, using the internet, connecting into work apps from a distance, and maintaining passwords are established by a cybersecurity policy.

Businesses may effectively spread the word about cybersecurity by outlining the best practices for acts like the ones stated above, advocating those practices, and explaining the impact and potential consequences of not adhering to the best practices.

5. Engage learners in cybersecurity training programs

Frequent cybersecurity training sessions may be implemented more successfully by making sure the information is engaging. If employees go through repetitive training programs that are made up only of textual content or PowerPoint slides, they could lose interest in cybersecurity. The addition of video content, game learning through interactive activities/competitions among employees, or the implementation of a reward system for accurately recognizing dangers can all significantly boost the effectiveness of cybersecurity training programs. These techniques can all improve the programs' engagement and raise people's awareness of cybersecurity.

6. Focus on ensuring that senior management promotes cybersecurity

Senior management of a corporation should be a model for strong cybersecurity practices. By acting in a way that is expected of staff members, leadership may set the tone and standard for the entire business and promote a culture of cybersecurity awareness.

7. Make sure training is focused and accessible.

Instead of informing the entire cohort, it is critical to just inform the employees who would be affected by the threat. Sending confusing and pointless information about cyber threats in an effort to increase cybersecurity awareness could be counterproductive. Making sure that communications are uncomplicated, concise, and clear is also essential. The efficiency of cybersecurity training can be increased by removing technical language because not every employee is an IT professional.

ADVANTAGES OF CYBER SECURITY AWARENESS ACROSS FIRMS AND ORGANIZATIONS

Awareness

Human error plays a huge part in cyberattacks. Employee expertise is essential for efficient security. Employees that are familiar with cybersecurity have the assurance to spot security dangers when they happen and are aware of how to respond and escalate problems.

Reduction of the threat

Knowledge of cybersecurity is crucial for lowering the risks that could lead to data breaches and other cybersecurity problems. The use of social media, email, and websites that are often accessed at work will raise workers' understanding of information security best practices.

Downtime will be avoided

It may cost a lot of money and take some time to remediate a breach or other security catastrophe before normal corporate activities can be resumed. Employees who are knowledgeable about cybersecurity ideas and are conscious of their roles in keeping your company secure are significantly less likely to be the victim of a cyberattack, and essential business processes can continue.

Compliance

Deeply knowledgeable employees in cybersecurity will be familiar with compliance regulations and understand how to handle sensitive data and information, enhancing your company's security and assisting your compliance efforts.

BENEFITS OF CYBERSECURITY

Cyber security is currently getting a lot of attention as a result of the rising use of the internet and computers by the media, as well as by governmental and commercial entities. They are aware of the devastation that cyberattacks may cause. Cyber-attacks are currently creating threat, destruction, and disruption on a global scale through computer-based criminal behavior. Foreign cyberattacks are on the rise as more people use the internet globally and there is no worldwide legal framework for cyberspace.

Preventative measures against information theft and attack are part of cybersecurity. The prevalence of computer crime and cyberattacks has increased since the introduction of information systems. A cyberattack uses a computer and a network.

Cybercrime has spread as widely and far as technology and the Internet. All kinds of businesses and organizations need information technology security solutions due to the increased adoption of the internet and digital technologies.

Let's find out what advantages cyber security has and how organizations all around the world profit from it.

- **It will protect your business** - The key benefit of using the best IT security cyber security solutions is that they may offer comprehensive digital protection for your company. This allows employees to browse the internet at their discretion while also protecting them from harm.

- **Safeguards Personal Data**: One of the most valuable commodities in today's technologically advanced world is personal information. It's possible that a virus will sell the information it gathers about your clients or staff members or, if it can, use it to steal their money.

- **Preserves and Boosts Productivity**: When viruses invade your systems and network, they will cease to function, making further work all but impossible. In reality, this will cause your team's downtime at work, waste, and the closure of the entire enterprise. It is still working well.

- **Prevents website crashes**: If your business is small, it's likely that you host your website. If your system gets infected, there is a good probability that your website will have to go down. This suggests that in addition to the losses resulting from missing transactions, you also run the danger of losing the patrons' trust, and some infections may lead to long-term system harm.
- **Assistance for Your IT Professional**: When it comes to thwarting cyberattacks and thieves, a strong security system frequently gives your company and employees the best tools, methods, and assistance.

DISADVANTAGES OF CYBER SECURITY

A priceless tool called cyber security is currently used to preserve and protect the most cutting-edge methods of conducting business. Simply described, cyber security refers to a set of procedures used to gain access to, alter, or destroy user data, extract money from users, or hinder normal corporate operations.

Cyber security has limitations even though it is essential for building a secure digital environment.

Let's discuss a few cyber security disadvantages to learn more about the field's applicability to organizations.

The High -Cost of Cyber Security

For some firms, cybersecurity may be too expensive. Businesses that lack the means to appropriately safeguard their information and IT infrastructure may suffer. Businesses frequently have to spend more money on cybersecurity than they generate in revenue. This is one of the key causes why so many organizations are reluctant to invest in cybersecurity.

The complexity of computer security

The complexity of cybersecurity may be too much for enterprises or organizations to handle. Security measures implementation takes a lot of effort and time. Even some organizations may find it too difficult to comprehend. This could lead to a number of issues at work. Data loss or even a security breach could result from the company's lack of adequate security procedures.

The requirement for ongoing supervision

For cybersecurity, ongoing observation is required. A company's entire system's cybersecurity needs to be continuously maintained, especially in light of the fact that hackers and cybercriminals are constantly developing new methods of breaking into a company's network. The greatest technique to maintain any system secure and up to date is also continual monitoring. This remains the best course of action for preserving security and functioning.

The lifelong process as the field characteristic

Cybersecurity is a continual process that is maintained by constant updates and enhancements. You cannot simply set cybersecurity in place and walk away from it. Years must pass between planning and implementation. Additionally, the security measures in place must be regularly reviewed and improved. If you want to gain from cybersecurity, you must continue to invest in it.

Risks to cyber security can be extremely high

Businesses may find cybersecurity to be too dangerous. Businesses frequently hold off on implementing effective cybersecurity measures out of concern that doing so might imperil their data and lead to security breaches, which might cost them a lot of money, harm their reputation, and even drive away customers.

In general, the following are disadvantages of cyber security:

- User access to certain Internet activity may be restricted by improperly constructed firewalls until the firewall is properly set.
- Proper firewall configuration can be difficult.
- Slows down the system's performance compared to before
- The price may be too much for the average user..
- To maintain security, the new application needs to be updated periodically.

THE SIGNIFICANCE OF CYBER SECURITY IN OUR LIFE

Everyone who uses the internet is at risk due to the increase in cyberattacks. Not just big corporations are targeted.

Online cyberattacks provide a challenge because the hacker may be based quite far from our physical location, perhaps even on another continent. But we also need to protect ourselves from other threats besides hackers. The maximum degree of caution is required when dealing with other types of cyber fraud.

Because of this, possessing cybersecurity abilities is becoming more and more crucial for all users who utilize any kind of account to engage online.

The Cyber Security Breaches Survey (2019) estimates that cyberattacks cost the UK billions of pounds annually. Regardless of their size, over 43% of firms have reported at least one hack in the last 12 months, putting them into context.

Any organization must have a cybersecurity strategy in place, especially as the world gets more and more digital. Since cyberattacks are only anticipated to increase in frequency and sophistication, those that haven't made the necessary investments in cybersecurity solutions in 2022 will be at a huge disadvantage.

Of these, 74% of the organizations reported that cybersecurity was their top concern. The issue is made worse by the fact that these harmed firms only use simple software.

Hackers are growing more intelligent, and they use a variety of methods or software weaknesses in addition to being intelligent people. Of course, a hacker rarely works alone; instead, an entire team methodically plans out a cyber-attack.

Despite the fact that the largest companies generally employ the most skilled cyber security professionals, there is a danger that the information could one day be misused because of a bug in a paid service that isn't necessarily their own.

There have been cases where a cyberattack was launched not with the intention of making money but with the satisfaction of inflicting local or global damage.

Nowadays, most people access the Internet using at least one smart device, whether they are online consumers or operators of online businesses. Therefore, if it is not properly maintained and protected, it makes for an excellent target for cybercriminals. Over 21 billion devices are expected to be online by 2021, increasing the number of possible targets for hackers.

Most of us regularly use smartphones, laptops, home routers, smart TVs, high-end cars, DVRs, and cameras, among other gadgets, to connect to the Internet.

While having access to the Internet enables us to carry out activities like online shopping, bill payment, watching movies and music, using maps, and more. Even more connected home products are now possible thanks to IoT (Internet of Things), including lighting, thermostats, Amazon Echo devices, and more.

Unfortunately, many of these linked devices won't be constructed with security in mind, which will lead to brand-new problems for everyone's online security. Millions of homes have already experienced power outages due to attacks on industrial control systems (ICS), such as water treatment and power grids, or illnesses brought on by untreated germs.

Therefore, it is advised that all online businesses implement all practical security measures and give them increased priority, including safeguarding email accounts with strong passwords, installing SSL certificates for secure connections, using hosting services that ensure server security, using antivirus and antispam software, and last but not least, employee training.

POSSIBLE CAREER OPTIONS IN CYBERSECURITY

The world has been taken over by technology, which is clear from our daily activities and from how businesses across all sectors operate now as opposed to a decade ago. The adoption of technology and digitization have grown exponentially, particularly since the Covid-19 pandemic. Today, technology is practically present in all areas of our existence.

Fraudulent activities including phishing, data breaches, hacking, money laundering, and other cybercrimes have expanded along with the rise in technology utilization.

Due to this, cybersecurity is now essential to efficient and secure corporate operations. Professionals in the growingly important field of cybersecurity are in high demand right now.

These job options are available to you if you work in cyber security:

SECURITY SOFTWARE DEVELOPER

During the design and development phase, security software developers create security software and incorporate security into applications software. A security software developer may manage a group of developers in the creation of secure software tools, develop an organization-wide software security strategy, take part in the lifecycle development of software systems, support software deployments to customers, and test their work for vulnerabilities, depending on the particular position and company.

HOW TO ADVANCE IN THIS CAREER

Strong technology background

A background in both cybersecurity and computer programming is necessary for this vocation.

Typically, this education begins with coursework in college or relevant work experience in software engineering or development. For this kind of employment, previous experience dealing with security concerns is also crucial to professional advancement. When attempting to anticipate potential issues and solutions for product development, practical experience dealing with cybersecurity threats becomes extremely important.

Working with actual security risks through corporate cybersecurity departments, consultants, or within a security operations center is the greatest method to gain expertise and background in the sector.

Working with teams

Working in a team is another crucial aspect of developing security software. It's crucial to acquire abilities that will facilitate collaboration and communication while honing technical know-how and experience with security threat detection and eradication.

Future career chances will also be aided by developing a professional network and developing a reputation as a team member.

WHAT IS A SECURITY SOFTWARE DEVELOPER?

Software engineers must possess creativity, be goal-oriented, and have a strong drive to create the best solution possible despite numerous challenges and divergent objectives. Developers of security software must go one step further and guarantee that the finished software is also secure from external threats.

This requires a creative individual who can envisage hazards both now and shortly.

Additionally, deadline pressure is a common issue for security software developers. They are working to ensure that all of the project's objectives and components are accomplished. Then, they must ensure that it functions as intended.

The need to balance product speed and functionality with security is one of the main issues faced by makers of security software. In other words, the product development and engineering teams must weigh the potential impact of introducing security restrictions on the user experience of the final product. There is much to overcome.

SKILLS AND EXPERIENCE IN DEVELOPING SECURITY SOFTWARE

- A bachelor's degree in computer science or a closely related subject, including electrical engineering, computer networking, or computer engineering.

- The creation or engineering of software. It is frequently necessary to have prior coding and programming skills.

- Professional experience in cybersecurity. A network security engineer is a good field to work in, whether as a cybersecurity engineer or a consultant.

- Training and certifications. Security or software vendors provide a wide range of certifications and training programs, including Microsoft AZURE Security Associate, Cisco CCIE, and CISSP. They are numerous. Even just obtaining these credentials can result in wage rises.

- Auditing and testing expertise. Experience testing and auditing software (such as experience as a penetration tester) for vulnerabilities is another important ability for security software engineers.

WHAT DO SECURITY SOFTWARE DEVELOPERS DO?

In 2015, two computer hackers targeted a Jeep Cherokee as it was traveling down the highway as part of an experiment for wired magazine. The assailants were able to activate the air conditioner and windshield wipers before finally being able to switch off the Jeep's engine and bring it to a stop. What makes it interesting? They were kilometers away from the truck when the attack took place, demonstrating the strength and potential of a focused cyber-attack.

This experiment is being conducted to demonstrate the susceptibility of internet-connected or internet-of-things (IoT) devices, even if they are as smart and massive as a Jeep Cherokee.

One excellent possibility for a security software developer is to comprehend and counteract threats to connected gadgets.

Similar to many IoT devices already on the market, the manufacturer didn't pay much attention to security when creating these computer interfaces. Maximum functionality, speed to market, and cost were the objectives. Security was a secondary concern.

In the upcoming years, there will be a rising number of chances for developers of security software that will necessitate enhancing the security of software-based goods and services. Before a product is released to the market, security developers must foresee these kinds of dangers and incorporate design features to guarantee safety and security and subsequently evaluate their effectiveness and efficiency.

SECURITY SOFTWARE DEVELOPER JOB DESCRIPTION

It is frequently necessary for security software development to collaborate closely with a software development team to create specifications, test, and design software components that are as secure as is practical. To ensure that potential risks are recognized and successfully addressed, communication with a team of engineers, designers, and developers is a crucial aspect of the process.

Software engineers are frequently tasked with producing ground-breaking technical designs and, occasionally, with completely new security software creations.

A critical step in the development process is testing and integrating cutting-edge systems and security measures to confirm the efficacy of the product design. These systems require in-depth expertise in software design and development, as well as dealing with architectures that have been hardened to defend against any future threats.

For this position, you must be creative and mentally sharp to consider every imaginable circumstance. Moreover, to simultaneously fully integrate it into the architecture you mentioned. These software roles occasionally require analysts to look at defenses and countermeasures. Security software engineers occasionally take part in red team-style exercises to test their products for the required defenses. These contentious situations can be very exciting.

Security-conscious developers need to be aware of potential attack surfaces and attack channels. Then, utilizing testing and red team methodologies to uncover these issues, they must be able to establish whether these attack routes will be susceptible to an exploit.

SECURITY ARCHITECT

Organizations demand qualified employees to assist them stay up with their expanding security requirements in the rapidly evolving sector of cybersecurity. The people in charge of these tasks are security architects. A security architect is needed to supervise the creation of a new network and ensure that security measures are implemented as soon as possible. A network could not be constructed without taking the required security precautions into account, and the business would fail.

Efficiency is frequently thought to be killed by security. Security architects are in charge of making sure that this is not the case in their networks. Deploying security measures that don't affect the network's overall effectiveness and efficiency is crucial.

Security architects will manage both defensive and offensive actions on the network. Knowing about firewalls, penetration testing, and incident response are only the beginning. It will also be necessary to have substantial computer networking understanding, such as routing and switching, because security architects will help build networks.

People who are interested in networking, security, and a little bit of administration may do best as security architects.

STEPS TO FOLLOW WHEN PURSUING A CAREER AS A SECURITY ARCHITECT

1. Prepare: A security architect's position is typically not entry-level. Security architects should have five to 10 years of experience, at least some of which should be in the field of cybersecurity, according to New Horizons Computer Learning Center.

This suggests that those who choose this career path must be prepared for a difficult journey. One can prepare for a career as a security architect by choosing the type of degree they wish to pursue. Degrees in both conventional computer science and cybersecurity are both applicable in this field. The type of stepping stone work that will enable professionals to gain the required experience should then be chosen. All of this should be investigated in order to create a special career plan.

2. Learn: To become a security architect, students should first seek a bachelor's degree in a relevant discipline. The decision to enroll in a program that will progress one's career is up to the individual. For example, earning a bachelor's degree in cybersecurity or computer science would both be wise moves. Since a security architect is regarded as a management-level post, individuals will likely also need a master's degree in cybersecurity or a related field. Experience in comparable fields can occasionally be used in place of a master's degree.

3. Gain Experience: It was already known that a security architect's position is not entry-level. This suggests that those who desire to work as security architects will likely need to begin their careers in another position. People typically start off in entry-level positions, move up to upper middle-level positions, and then transition into the role of a security architect because it is a management post.

For instance, a person may begin their career as a system administrator in the security industry, move up to the position of security engineer, and then be able to move into the role of security architect. Additional jobs that could be good starting points for a career as a security architect include security administrator, network administrator, security expert, security analyst, and security consultant.

4. Pursue Certifications: As is the case with the majority of cybersecurity professions, certifications can help professionals and students showcase their abilities and set their resumes apart from the competition. The CompTIA Security+ certification is a superb entry-level certificate for anyone with an interest in cybersecurity. This certification covers both hypothetical and actual cybersecurity scenarios.

To pursue more advanced or expert-level certifications, professionals may focus on earning their CISSP. The prerequisites for CISSP certification include in-depth and practical understanding of cybersecurity topics such security and risk management, asset security, security architecture and engineering, IAM, security assessment and testing, security operations, and software development security. A few examples of intermediate certificates that fall somewhere between the Security+ and the CISSP skill levels are the Certified Ethical Hacker (CEH), the Offensive Security Certified Professional (OSCP), and the Certified Cloud Security Professional (CCSP).

5. Apply: After researching security architects, earning the necessary degree and credentials, and gaining 5 to 10 years of experience in a related field, there is only one thing left to accomplish. Like any other career in the industry, jobs in cybersecurity may be found online by searching for terms like "security architect" on websites like Indeed.com, Glassdoor.com, LinkedIn, and many others.

6. Keep Learning: A security architect is always picking up new skills. As managers in a field where security is constantly changing, security architects must routinely stay up to date on new and developing threats and security techniques. Attending training sessions provided by organizations like Black Hat and SANs may make it easier for security architects to keep up with current information.

WHAT IS A SECURITY ARCHITECT?

Security architects are management-level people who manage network security. These specialists are needed at the start of the network's design, building, and implementation as well as for the duration of the network's existence. Security architects will be in charge of overseeing any network modifications to make sure they don't endanger the company.

Security architects usually manage both offensive testing, such as conducting penetration tests, and defensive measures, such as setting up and configuring firewalls and antivirus software.

SECURITY ARCHITECT SKILLS

Depending on the organization, different security architects will require different qualifications.

The following are the kinds of skills security architects should possess:

- **Networking:** Security architects will play a crucial role in the creation and upkeep of computer networks. As a result, security architects need to have a profound understanding of the principles of computer networking. Being an authority in computer networking should be the main priority for anyone looking to break into the industry.

- **Malware analysis:** To effectively protect the network against malware, a basic knowledge of malware and malware analysis is needed.

- **Management skills:** People interested in a career as a security architect must be capable of managing a project and a team of workers because this is a management role.

- **Risk management:** A security architect's responsibilities include a sizable portion of risk management, therefore understanding its fundamentals is crucial.

WHAT DO SECURITY ARCHITECTS DO?

Security architects are a key component of any IT project or endeavor that a firm undertakes. It will be necessary to plan, create, and maintain the security architectures that will be constructed around these projects or initiatives. To maintain the highest level of security for a business, they will do routine testing, occasionally involving tasks like penetration testing, vulnerability scanning, and risk analysis.

They will be knowledgeable about new developments in technology and vigilant about potential dangers so they can take precautions to fend off potential threats. They typically oversee and supervise the security personnel working for a company. Campaigns to raise awareness of security are typically under the direction of security architects.

SECURITY ARCHITECT JOB DESCRIPTION

Even though each job description will be particular to the hiring business, the fundamental qualifications and skills are frequently constant.

The following categories of items can be expected to appear on job descriptions for security architects:

- Managing and maintaining the security mechanisms in place for the system as well as putting new and enhanced systems into place.
- Ensure that the least privilege rule is followed by every employee.
- Perform security audits of third-party software and services.
- Implement and manage Identity & Access Management (IAM) security architecture.
- Managing and supervising programs for security awareness training;
- Managing ongoing security tests including vulnerability scanning and risk analysis.

SECURITY CONSULTANT

The responsibility of an information security consultant is to prevent unauthorized access to their client's networks and data. There are numerous positions in the field of information security, sometimes known as cybersecurity. Some have a broad range of general responsibilities. Others are extremely specialized and concentrated in a particular cybersecurity field. Although they may specialize in one or more areas, cybersecurity consultants often perform as generalists.

A security consultant may specialize in any of the positions listed below from George Washington University. Throughout their careers, the majority of security consultants will switch between some of these positions. A security consultant frequently performs multiple tasks at once (including many of the roles listed on the career hub).

PREPARING FOR A CAREER AS A SECURITY CONSULTANT

- Gain a basic understanding of networking - Security experts safeguard devices and data on a network. To be effective at security, you must have a solid understanding of networking.

- Understand the fundamentals of cybersecurity - You might be eager to discover how networks are breached, but take the time to comprehend the fundamentals.

- Develop your coding and/or scripting skills- good to know languages include Python, JavaScript, PowerShell, Node.js, Bash, Ruby, and Perl.

- Create a lab - Book knowledge by itself won't equip you with the necessary skills. Additionally crucial is having first-hand experience. People who are interested in building a home lab should receive some instruction. Don't be put off by the word "lab." A quality lab can be constructed for a reasonable cost and with few resources.

- Obtaining certification is a little challenging. You can choose from a wide variety of cybersecurity qualifications, and you never know which one a potential employer will favor. For some qualifications, there are free online courses available, but the examinations themselves are highly pricey. Many businesses may compensate staff members for additional education and certification. Having cybersecurity knowledge and abilities on display is far more crucial than being certified. Your abilities will land you the job; after that, seek certification.

WHAT IS A SECURITY CONSULTANT?

An information security consultant with training in maintaining the confidentiality, integrity, and availability of data and network devices is a security consultant. To offer such security, there are numerous options. If Mary and Mark work as cybersecurity consultants, Mary might be a security architect, creating security controls for a variety of clients' businesses, and Mark might be a security administrator, setting up and managing security systems for his own business.

Security consultants may be employed by companies or operate independently. Security device configuration may be the initial task for entry-level consultants. An organization's security strategy can be created and implemented with the aid of a virtual chief information security officer (vCISO), who has years of expertise in advanced roles.

The true definition of a hacker is someone who is curious and learns how to use technology to solve issues. Cybersecurity experts fall into this category. They naturally pursue lifelong learning, which is a crucial quality for the following reasons:

- As threats evolve, the security environment is continuously shifting. Attackers frequently adapt their techniques.

- Because technology advances so quickly, education and protection must also keep up. One such is cloud computing, which necessitates a distinct security strategy from on premise security.

- Organizations are requesting more effective security solutions than ever before due to the rise in catastrophic breaches.

SECURITY CONSULTANT SKILLS AND EXPERIENCE

A successful security consultant must possess both hard and soft talents. It is tempting to emphasize technical expertise while downplaying the value of soft competencies. Do not commit that error!

The soft and technical skills on this list are those that are commonly expected of information security consultants.

Technical Skills

- Must possess a solid understanding of IT infrastructure architecture.

- Security certifications such as CISA, CISM, CISSP, and CGEIT.

- Experience advising clients on architecture meetings industry standards such as PCI DSS, ISO 27001, HIPAA, and GDPR.

- Experience working with firewalls, load balancers, proxies, VPNs, and endpoint security tools. Platforms for AV, IPS, SSL inspection, SIEM, or security monitoring

- Strong understanding of network architecture, topology, and the OSI Layer 7 model.

Soft Skills

- Project management expertise, including the capacity to drive projects to completion and uphold deadlines.
- Excellent communication, writing, and presentation abilities are required.
- You must also be clever, persuasive, and able to serve as a valuable counsel to the top client security leadership.
- Ability to travel to customer sites as necessary.
- Demonstrated ability to think strategically about business, product, and technical difficulties.
- Should be able to explain security-related concepts to a wide variety of technical and non-technical people.

WHAT DO SECURITY CONSULTANTS DO?

The never-ending fight is for accuracy, justice, and cybersecurity consulting. Putting exaggeration aside, security experts do engage in a never-ending arms race with malevolent hackers who are the bad guys.

Security consultants, at their most basic level, make the internet and company networks safer places. They provide security controls to guard against breaches by planning, designing, constructing, configuring, coding, running, maintaining, and/or overseeing them. It's a mouthful, but it might have easily been longer.

Security experts take measures to make it difficult for anyone to access data or network devices without authorization and to cause harm. The options for doing this are virtually endless. They can be divided into three broad categories: response, detection, and prevention. While security consultants handling detection and response may code and monitor, that handling prevention may plan, implement, and configure security safeguards.

Mary, the security architect, comes to mind. She takes care of defense. Before her arrival, her organization experienced a significant data breach. An administrator account that simply required a username and password that were compromised were utilized by the attacker to gain access to the system. Mary was now in charge of stopping future assaults like that one.

She evaluated the current security measures and created a new set of measures that she thought would be more efficient. She started by making all administrator accounts subject to multifactor authentication. In other words, access to those accounts required more than simply a password. That will stop an attack like the one they had previously.

The security administrator, Mark, was focusing on detection. To find questionable attempts to access computers, he installed security monitoring. His firewall configuration of tougher access rules contributed to prevention as well. Therefore, security consultants can play a variety of functions, and they often do.

SECURITY CONSULTANT JOB DESCRIPTION

We now know that the responsibilities of security consultants might change depending on the position. Job descriptions will therefore differ as well. However, some components are included in numerous job descriptions. Let's dissect the Senior Security Consultant job description that Amazon Web Services advertised on Indeed.

- 3+ years of experience working with security and compliance standards

Standards and compliance play a significant role in security. Typically, security measures must adhere to regulations like PCI DSS, ISO 27001, HIPAA, or GDPR. These and other requirements will be demanded of security consultants.

- Technical training or related experience

The analysis shows that not all jobs necessitate a college degree. In either case, candidates must be able to show that they have the knowledge and abilities that come from experience.

- A highly technical subject matter expert who can delve deeply and collaborate with clients to meet the security, risk, and compliance requirements of their AWS migrations is needed for this post.

The explanation: The term "subject matter expert" suggests that you have extensive knowledge in a certain field. However, you still require broad networking skills in addition to a depth of understanding across a variety of security areas.

- You'll like developing cloud solutions for a variety of challenging intelligence community clients while also instructing, training, and designing them. You will like retaining your present technical knowledge and gaining new ones so you can make a major contribution to in-depth discussions on architecture.

The breakdown: Technical knowledge and abilities alone are insufficient. A security team requires cooperation from all members. The best way to succeed is to teach others and share your expertise.

- Consultants may be required to travel to clients' locations as needed (50–75%) to provide their services.

The breakdown: Travel is a need for most consulting positions. Determine how much travel is permissible and confirm that you are aware of the requirements for each position.

- Comprehensive knowledge of migration issues and cloud computing technologies. Professional expertise in designing, installing, and running AWS-based solutions.

The breakdown: Since AWS is a cloud computing environment, familiarity with this field is necessary. However, because of how quickly businesses are adopting cloud computing, most cybersecurity professionals require some familiarity with this field.

- Software/technology sales consulting experience, or comparable qualifications.

The breakdown: Some security consultants assist in the sales of security goods and services provided by their business.

This is only one illustration. Coding or scripting is a talent that is frequently needed but is not specifically included in this job description. PowerShell, Python, Node.js, Javascript, Bash, Ruby, and Perl are examples of commonly needed software. Project management skill is also demanded.

INFORMATION SECURITY ANALYST

The first line of defense for networks is provided by information security analysts, who install firewalls and encrypt data to prevent intrusions and continuously monitor and audit systems for odd behavior.

A security analyst is someone whose primary responsibility is to keep an eye on computer networks and infrastructure to make sure they are secure.

A security analyst's duties may include managing firewalls and network updates, restricting file access and credentialing, aggressively attempting to hack systems to discover flaws and more.

A bachelor's degree in cybersecurity, information security, or a similar discipline, like those required for other cybersecurity sector job titles, is the finest preparation for a security analyst. Candidates for cybersecurity analyst employment are also helped in their search by professional, industry-recognized certifications, work experience, and internships.

FOUR STEPS TO BECOMING A SECURITY ANALYST

1. **Research**: The good news is that there are many employment chances for cybersecurity professionals to position themselves properly as the number of opportunities and new types of occupations that come under the cybersecurity analyst position category continue to increase. Therefore, the first step in becoming a cybersecurity analyst is to identify the type of job you want to accomplish and then link that to the training and credentials you will require. It's wise to prepare ahead of time because even entry-level security analyst employment could need specialized training.

2. **Education**: The majority of cybersecurity analysts hold a bachelor's degree in cybersecurity, according to the Bureau of Labor Statistics (BLS) (or a closely related field such as mathematics, computer science, or engineering). However, in some cases, security professionals with associate's degrees and/or relevant training or background (such as military service, for example) can gain entry-level cybersecurity jobs in the private sector with the right cybersecurity certifications (see the following point).

3. **Certification**: One factor that distinguishes cybersecurity from other professions is the fact that many jobs, both entry-level and mid-career, call for some sort of certification that demonstrates mastery of a certain skill. It is best practice to pay attention to what kinds of certifications are necessary for different occupations within the sector when preparing for a career in cybersecurity. Check out our certification guide for additional details on cybersecurity certifications.

4. **Network**: Creating a professional network is crucial to becoming a security analyst. Maintaining knowledge of the most recent trends and opportunities in the field will be facilitated by a network that is oriented toward a particular career path.

WHAT IS A SECURITY ANALYST?

Working with a variety of computer and information networks is possible for security analysts. Security analysts can be found wherever there are vast amounts of data being kept, exchanged, or used by a computer, including business databases, banking networks, office networks, and military intelligence. An experienced security analyst will likely be knowledgeable about advanced hardware, software, and data management and storage concepts.

Ransomware attacks, social engineering assaults, and the theft or compromise of critical information from within a corporation or organization are the top three cybersecurity dangers to information technology networks of all sizes. The implication of this is that cybersecurity analysts must be equipped to handle a wide range of threats and search for security concerns both internally and externally.

SECURITY ANALYST SKILLS AND EXPERIENCE

The knowledge and abilities needed for cybersecurity will differ greatly between jobs. Some security analyst job listings are looking for candidates with particular expertise, such as administering a private network, instructing new hires, or performing penetration testing on the company's online assets.

Studying a variety of job descriptions at various firms is a critical strategy for students and early career professionals to determine what the most valuable and marketable work abilities are. Trends and the relationship between opportunities and the present skill set and expertise should start to emerge from this research. Making judgments regarding the security certifications and degrees to seek will also be aided by having a thorough understanding of the work market.

Despite the great variety of positions available for cybersecurity analysts, there are a few traits or abilities that are typical in the industry:

- Proven programming skills. Since cybersecurity analysts are responsible for protecting digital infrastructure, it makes sense that cybersecurity professionals should be knowledgeable in foundational programming languages like C, C++, PHP, Perl, and Java as well as some basic programming knowledge.

- Analytical. Security analysts must be able to draw knowledge from multiple sources because they work with data from a range of sources.

- Detail-oriented. The majority of the work done by cybersecurity analysts involves looking at minute elements, such as computer code or network commands, that might have significant effects.

- Forward-thinking. Security analysts must project future events using data and trends from the present and then recommend appropriate security measures.

WHAT DO SECURITY ANALYSTS DO?

In a group or business, a security analyst frequently serves in a variety of roles. They could be a mix of a trainer or instructor, a designer of systems, a maker of policies, and a police officer.

As they are frequently called upon to triage security incidents, security analysts could be considered the first responders of the digital world. However, in actuality, the majority of cybersecurity analysts spend their time developing policies and procedures, reviewing best practices, and offering training to staff members of businesses or organizations.

In a perfect world, a security analyst would be proactive in preventing security breaches before they happen. That can entail updating systems and software often, or it might entail actively trying to breach firewalls or uncover security holes in operating systems or computer code.

SECURITY ANALYST JOB DESCRIPTION

A simple scan of a few of the hundreds of job descriptions for security analysts reveals that the positions offered range from entry-level to more specialized security and threat mitigation professionals.

The California Employment Development Department has published some basic information about what some of the common job criteria are for cybersecurity analyst employment, despite the great variability in the precise skills and certifications needed for different occupations.

- Create and maintain firewalls and encrypt data transmissions to safeguard private data.
- Create strategies and technologies to safeguard computer data and files from accidental erasure or change caused by malware or other attack vectors.
- Create strategies and protocols for responding to data breaches and assaults.
- Keep up with the most recent attack vectors and create methods to defend against them.
- Keep track of computer software and user activity to safeguard networks and corporate data.
- Create and implement routine risk assessments to make sure security best practices are followed.
- Discuss security issues with coworkers and educate them on how to network and data users can strengthen individual and group information security.

ETHICAL HACKERS

Ethical hackers typically possess a CEH accreditation, and their employers authorize them to attempt to breach the security of their system. The plan is to test current security protocols using the same methods employed by malicious black hat hackers; if they are effective, new security measures can be created and put into place.

Whitehat hackers and blackhat hackers, respectively, have historically been used to refer to defensive and offensive cybersecurity endeavors. To distinguish between the good guys and the bad guys, these nicknames were utilized. Although both of these phrases are still often used, one of them could not sufficiently describe the numerous responsibilities present in the modern cybersecurity ecosystem today.

The good guys are now better identified by terms like the red team, blue team, purple team, ethical hacker, and penetration tester, even though a black hat hacker is still just the bad guy. Red teams especially offer offensive security services, while blue teams offer defensive ones. Teams that offer some of each type of security service are identified by the color purple, which is created by combining the colors red and blue.

All security experts who offer offensive services, including red teams, pen testers, and independent offensive consultants, are referred to as ethical hackers. Other job titles that could contain inappropriate language are security analysts or engineers. These offensive security services are frequently grouped within a company's threat and vulnerability management organization.

These many terms for ethical hackers are used interchangeably in this book, even though there are some minor technical distinctions between, for example, the services offered by an independent offensive cybersecurity consultant and an internal pentester.

The main goal of an ethical hacker is to look at security from the viewpoint of the adversary to identify weaknesses that malicious users could take advantage of. This gives defense teams the chance to prepare by coming up with a patch before an actual attack can take place. Executing simulated cyberattacks in a safe setting helps to achieve this goal. While evaluating security measures and devices for perimeter penetration vulnerabilities makes up a large portion of the value that ethical hackers offer, they also search more generally for flaws that can be exploited deep within a network or application, such as data exfiltration vulnerabilities.

ROLE OF AN ETHICAL HACKER

Ethical hackers can work as independent contractors, as in-house security guards for a company's website or apps, or as simulated offensive cybersecurity specialists for a company. All of these career choices need an understanding of current attack techniques and tools, although the in-house ethical hacker may only need to be well-versed in a specific class of software or digital asset.

An in-house red team may have the advantage of having deeper expertise in their systems and applications than an independent consultant, despite being a relatively new concept in the security business. The red team has an advantage thanks to this insider information, so long as they can keep from being too narrow-minded in their thinking. Real attackers would need several years to duplicate this edge. Most people believe that internal teams are less expensive overall than hiring a consulting agency on an ongoing basis.

On the other hand, an advantage that an external ethical hacker might offer is a fresh pair of eyes to spot vulnerabilities that the internal team might have missed. Even companies with an internal red team may periodically hire an outside ethical hacker to give their defenses a new perspective.

Before initiating any offensive activity, the client's written consent is especially crucial for any external offensive security service provider. The systems, networks, apps, and websites that will be a part of the simulated attack should be specified in this permission. Without further explicit authorization, do not broaden the service's scope.

There are white-box, black-box, and gray-box ethical hacker engagements in line with the industry's use of colors to distinguish between different cybersecurity responsibilities and functions. Giving the security expert as much knowledge as they can about the target system and application is known as a "white-box engagement." As a result, the simulated assault may swiftly search wide and deep for weaknesses that would take a genuinely bad actor a very long time to find.

In contrast, a black-box interaction occurs when the ethical hacker receives no insider information. This more accurately represents the circumstances of an actual attack and might give important information about what a potential attack vector would resemble. The simulation of an attack in which the attacker has already breached the perimeter and possibly spent some time inside the system or application is known as a "gray-box engagement," as the name suggests.

All three engagement modes are frequently used by businesses along with internal and external ethical hackers. Although this type of applied knowledge is significantly more expensive to carry out, it can offer the clearest picture of what defenses need to be deployed.

For many additional security professions, having ethical hacking abilities and expertise is advantageous. For network security analysts and engineers, these abilities are essential. People with offensive skills are needed for purple teams. Application security developers gain from having a working knowledge of attack techniques and equipment. Security researchers, also referred to as bug hunters, rely heavily on their understanding of offensive strategies. Many successful bug hunters have knowledge that extends beyond the application layer to the network layer and other potentially vulnerable regions.

THE SKILLS REQUIRED TO BECOME AN ETHICAL HACKER

While anecdotal accounts of black hat hackers becoming white hats in the past abound, the most crucial qualification for being a successful ethical hacker today is to have, as the term suggests, high ethical standards. The difference between good and evil is ethics. Many black hat hackers possess the necessary technical expertise to operate ethically but lack the self-control of character to act morally no matter the alleged advantages of acting otherwise.

A cybersecurity team member runs an unacceptably high risk if they have a history of crimes. This kind of danger would be unthinkable for a huge company with a knowledgeable legal team. So, a word of advice: if you're an ethical hacker seeking a job, don't include any work on your resume that even remotely suggests illegal or unethical activity because it will get you quickly disqualified. While it's true that people can change over time, the majority of employers recognize that creating a set of moral principles for a living involves much more than simply wanting to change careers.

Second to covering the "ethical" component of this slang term is the requirement to also cover the "hacker" component. Advanced cybersecurity technological skills must be displayed by an applicant for an ethical hacker position. An element of the intended experience is the capacity to suggest mitigation and remediation measures.

An applicant must comprehend both wired and wireless networks to become an ethical hacker. They need to be skilled with many operating systems, particularly Windows and Linux. They must comprehend file systems and firewalls. They must be knowledgeable about servers, workstations, and computer science in general, as well as how file permissions operate.

Direct, manual, and hands-on assault tactics must be well understood and demonstrated, and strong coding abilities are a requirement. In other words, an ethical hacker should have protected so many assets during their career that copying the opponent and then anticipating their moves should come naturally to them.

A unique blend of creative and analytical thinking goes beyond sound moral principles and superior technical abilities. The ability to think like the enemy is a must for ethical hackers. They need to know what drives the bad guys and be able to gauge how much time and effort the blackhat could be prepared to devote to any given target. The pen tester must comprehend the worth of the data and the systems they safeguard to do this.

ETHICAL HACKER CERTIFICATIONS AND EDUCATION

Certified Ethical Hacker (CEH) and Offensive Security Certified Professional are the two credentials that are specifically related to ethical hacking (OSCP).

"A Certified Ethical Hacker is a trained professional who comprehends and knows how to look for weaknesses and vulnerabilities in target machine and uses the same tools and knowledge as a malicious hacker, but lawfully and legitimately to assess the security posture of a target system," according to EC-Council, which administers the CEH certification (s). From a vendor-neutral standpoint, the CEH certificate certifies persons in the unique network security discipline of ethical hacking.

Obtaining any of the additional cybersecurity professional certifications provided by the EC-Council will increase your employability as an ethical hacker.

According to Offensive Security, the OSCP exam consists of a virtual network with targets that have different operating systems and configurations. The exam and connectivity instructions are given to the student at the beginning of the exam for a separate exam network about which they are completely unfamiliar.

The candidate who passes the test will have proven their capacity to investigate the network (information gathering), spot any weaknesses, and carry out attacks. Frequently, this entails changing exploit code to infiltrate the systems and obtain administrator access.

A thorough penetration test report with detailed comments and screenshots outlining the results is required from the candidate. Depending on how tough they were to breach and how much access was gained, each compromised server receives points.

The best place to start your career is with a bachelor's degree in an area that involves computers. A preferred background for work in the security industry is one in computer science or network engineering. Give good multidisciplinary programs preference while looking at bachelor's degree programs in cybersecurity.

Good programs will have a strong emphasis on business management, computer science, and engineering. Look for schools that include classes in technical writing, as well as legal and ethical concerns related to technology. The best cybersecurity experts are well-rounded people who can view their industry from a broad perspective.

To stay up to date on contemporary assault techniques and offensive plans, self-study is required, even with a degree and one or more professional certifications. A home lab has several benefits. Successful ethical hackers use a variety of tactics to stay one step ahead of black hat hackers, including

YouTube tutorials, online organizations and forums, and posts and exchanges on social media.

HOW TO GET EXPERIENCE AS AN ETHICAL HACKER

Ethical hackers benefit greatly from prior exposure to vulnerability testing software like Metasploit, Netsparker, and OpenVAS. These and other resources are made to speed up the process of looking for known vulnerabilities. These or similar tools might offer a helpful framework for vulnerability scanning and management, but they shouldn't serve as an ethical hacker's starting point. The target must also be the target of manual simulated attacks. It is crucial to have knowledge about and experience with how these attacks are conducted.

Working for many years as a defensive security team member is nearly always a must on the road to becoming an ethical hacker. Most often, promotion within the department results in assignment to a top offensive club. Additional experience and education will qualify a candidate for a position on one of the security specialty teams or work as a freelance consultant, frequently starting with work as a security specialist, security administrator, or security software developer.

Beneficial experience goes beyond prior IT security work. Other relevant talents include social engineering and physical penetration testing. The first step in many attacks is gathering intelligence through a protracted social engineering campaign. Understanding the complete threat landscape can be greatly aided by having a thorough understanding of social engineering methods and tactics.

Sometimes a physical intrusion into a server room or data center comes before a cyberattack. An ethical hacker will be able to recognize the types and methods that are most likely to be applied in a real event by understanding what physical assets are vulnerable.

Security specialists are preventing cybercriminals from using their old strategies, so they must become more inventive. To acquire information and launch cyberattacks, physical attacks—including the deployment of drones to sniff out vulnerable networks—are being used more regularly. For the most thorough threat analysis, an ethical hacker must plan for and practice using both conventional and unconventional attack paths.

TYPICAL ETHICAL HACKING ASSIGNMENTS

Threat modeling, security analyses, vulnerability threat assessments (VTA), and report writing are among the common tasks given to ethical hackers. The duties of this position will undoubtedly vary from firm to company, but the job description will almost always include these essentials.

Threat modeling

Through the process of detecting weaknesses and coming up with countermeasures to thwart attacks or lessen their impact, threat modeling helps to maximize network security. In the context of threat modeling, a threat is a possible or current unfavorable occurrence that could compromise the assets of the company and may be malevolent (such as a denial-of-service attack) or inadvertent (such as the failure of a computer hardware). An ethical hacker would aid in this process by offering a thorough analysis of potential malicious assaults and the effects they might have on the organization.

Effective threat modeling aims to determine where a system's security needs the most attention. This may alter as new information comes to light, as apps are added, withdrawn, or upgraded, and as changing user needs emerge. Threat modeling is an iterative process that involves defining assets, understanding what each application does concerning these assets, creating a security profile for each application, identifying potential threats, prioritizing potential threats, and recording negative events and the actions taken in each case.

The threat modeling can continue to be theoretical rather than post-mortem after an actual attack thanks to the ethical hacker's crucial role.

Security assessment

Security assessments are frequently given to an ethical hackers, whether they are pentesters or red team leaders. In a nutshell, an information security assessment measures the security posture of a system or organization based on risk. Security assessments are routine exercises that gauge a company's level of security readiness. They include checks for IT system and business process vulnerabilities and recommendations for activities to reduce the risk of future attacks.

Security evaluations can also be used to analyze how well security-related policies are followed. They can help highlight the need for extra or improved security training and aid to strengthen regulations intended to prevent social engineering. The security assessment is a key risk management tool, concluding in a report that details flaws and offers suggestions.

Vulnerability threat assessment

A vulnerability threat assessment is a procedure used to identify, quantify, and rank the threats that could potentially exploit a system's relevant vulnerabilities. The VTA is carried out to discover and correlate particular threats and vulnerabilities, while it is closely tied to a security assessment. The fundamental security assessment mentioned above is intended to find weaknesses and analyze the enterprise's security posture without regard to any particular threat. The VTA is more of a threat-based evaluation.

Information technology systems, energy supply systems, water supply systems, transportation systems, and communication systems are a few examples of systems for which vulnerability threat analyses should be carried out. Such evaluations might be carried out on behalf of a variety of different businesses, from tiny firms to significant regional or national infrastructure entities. Each of these system varieties and/or businesses will need an ethical hacker to carry out the VTA.

Report writing

Writing precise and concise professional reports is a critical skill for carrying out the tasks of an ethical hacker. The utility of gathering data, detecting vulnerabilities, and connecting threats are little if risk management leaders cannot understand the pertinent information. The red team's reports are frequently the catalyst for large security resource investments. Professionals in risk management must have complete faith in the data collected by ethical hackers in their company. In some instances, a company will hire an ethical hacker as an outside consultant to supply the data required to support security expenditures for senior management or the board of trustees. The report is the main deliverable and is quite significant in the field of security consulting.

Do not undervalue the value of business writing skills while thinking about potential professional certifications and educational possibilities to advance a career to include ethical hacking. An individual's career will advance above a peer who is otherwise equally qualified if they can write a report successfully.

ETHICAL HACKING IN REVIEW

Both participating in an internal red team and working as a freelance whitehat hacker are interesting careers. Operations-level jobs are widely sought after since they can bring about a certain level of esteem and prominence within the cybersecurity community. For networks, systems, and applications to be effectively protected, ethical hacker professions are essential. This knowledge is necessary for all national infrastructure organizations and to protect sensitive or vital data across all industries.

The phrase "ethical hacker" often seems contradictory. It suggests two competing ideas. One relates to having high moral standards, and the other to "hacking," which is frequently connected to illegal conduct. Although an offensive security specialist might be a better term to employ, an ethical hacker is frequently used to characterize this class of security experts since, let's face it, an ethical hacker sounds more enigmatic.

These positions are not for the unethical, and certainly not for anyone with a history of being a bad actor, whether or not the word "hacker" is mentioned in the job description. Ethical hackers must have access to sensitive data, the disclosure of which could be disastrous for the company. Government employees and contractors frequently need security clearances. A background investigation and an assessment of financial and social media records are required to obtain a security clearance.

Ethical hackers typically collaborate as a team, with the somewhat unusual exception of the independent freelance offensive cybersecurity consultant. If you're on a red team, your teammates will all be ethical hackers or pen testers with a similar level of expertise, and your team will be a part of the wider security division. The ethical hacker may be the lone member of a larger security team in a smaller organization where they play the only offensive function.

Success depends on having the capacity to work well with others on the team and to communicate clearly. An ethical hacker is not the archetypal young teenager working out of his parent's basement wearing a hoodie who has switched from wearing a black hat to a white one. She is frequently a professional with education, training, experience, skill, and articulation who is committed to making the world a safer place to live and work.

While there are stories in the history of self-taught, tenacious individuals who pulled themselves up by their digital bootstraps to the top of cybersecurity operations, the norm for ethical hackers is an education that includes at least a bachelor's degree and one or more specialized professional certifications. Successful ethical hackers frequently have years of demonstrating their mettle in software development and/or more traditional defensive security professions.

DIGITAL FORENSICS EXPERTS

When information is taken from a computer, network, web application, mobile phone, or other digital device, experts in digital forensics, often known as cybercrime forensics, are called in to conduct an investigation. The forensics team's duties include figuring out exactly what happened and how it happened, making an effort to retrieve and/or fix stolen or damaged data files, and collaborating with other information security specialists to make sure it doesn't happen again.

Experts in digital forensics also referred to as DFOR, are essential in reducing the damage caused by cybercrimes and recreating the crime to aid in the prosecution of offenders. They are the digital CSIs of the InfoSec world.

The successful conclusion of an investigation requires that law enforcement personnel always adhere to the letter of the law. For digital forensics specialists, following adequate evidence management protocols will be of the utmost importance. Governments or government contractors employ a large number of digital forensic specialists. The majority of these occupations require a security clearance.

FOUR STEPS TO BECOMING A DIGITAL FORENSICS EXPERT

1. **Education**: Numerous college degree programs are available that can be used to seek professions in digital forensics. These include cybersecurity, applied mathematics, computer science, computer engineering, and digital forensics. Master's degrees are required for some positions in digital forensics that are more specialized.

2. **Career path**: Entry-level positions in digital forensics are easily accessible and provide excellent pathways into the sector. Another viable alternative is to develop technical expertise prior to learning InfoSec expertise. Additionally in demand are information technology positions with a specific emphasis on cybersecurity. Software development is a different profession that can lead to a career in digital forensics.

3. **Professional certifications**: Employers may ask for a variety of professional credentials, and this is particularly true if you want to apply for specific federal jobs. There are several

different certificates that could be obtained for digital forensics. For jobs in digital forensics, some organizations now offer generally recognized certificates.

4. **Keep current**: As is the case with the majority of career tracks in cybersecurity, it's critical to stay current with advances in the industry. When an industry has a dedicated professional trade association, it is easier to keep knowledge and skills up to date with all of the most recent trends. One example of a group in the digital forensics sector is the High Technology Crime Investigation Association.

By providing proper continuing education, professional training, and competency testing in digital forensics, experts can also stay up to date. The Scientific Working Group on Digital Evidence (SWGDE) is another organization dedicated to maintaining the knowledge and expertise of experts in the field of cybercrime forensics. The SWGDE seeks to encourage free discussion among business associations and professionals.

WHAT IS A DIGITAL FORENSICS?

Professionals in digital forensics have many different job titles, but most of them are variants on a single subject. Digital forensics engineer, digital forensics investigator, digital forensics professional, digital forensics analyst, digital forensics examiner, digital forensics technician, and others are among the titles regularly used.

While job scope usually changes less than titles, it will undoubtedly be influenced by seniority and amount of experience. Experts in cybercrime forensics typically come into play following an information security breach. Now is the time to don your CSI trench coat and thoroughly examine the available evidence. Just digital trails, no gore, and blood.

DIGITAL FORENSICS DEGREE, SKILLS, AND EXPERIENCE

An essential phase in the investigation of digital crimes is the examination of computing equipment, including mobile devices, software, network traffic analysis, memory analysis, media analysis, databases, and internet of things (IoT) devices (and pretty much anything else). Therefore, experts in digital forensics need to be quite knowledgeable with a variety of these platforms.

Some of skill requirements that employers may notice include the following:

- Proficient use of research methods to locate specified electronic data
- In-depth understanding of technology, including knowledge of mobile operating systems, networks, and hardware
- Knowledge of exploit tactics as well as proficiency in the latest cyber forensics, response, and reverse engineering methodologies.
- Proven competence with a range of forensics applications and tools.
- The ability to decipher malicious software and cryptic code;

- Inventing original methods to speed up the collection of evidence.
- Basic office file password cracking and mobile device backups
- Correcting the metadata in documents created in Office and PDF
- The ability to efficiently leveraging encryption in both hardware and software

Understanding of particular programming languages, including:

- Python
- Bash
- PHP
- C, C+, C#
- Java

Employers frequently seek out these common professional certifications, such as those offered by the International Society of Forensic Computer Examiners (ISFCE), The International Association of Computer Investigative Specialists (IACIS), GIAC (Global Information Assurance Certification), Cellebrite, AccessData, Inspector, EnCase, Magnet, NUIX, and Truxton, (ISC)2 (International Information Systems Security Certification Consortium), IEEE, and others (Institute of Electronic and Electrical Engineers).

Moreover, some firms could require more fundamental certifications like CompTIA A+ or Net+, which are linked to technical support and operational IT skills. Additionally, there are training and certification programs that are much more specifically tailored to a single or select group of certain types of hardware or operating systems. This kind of training is called iOS Forensics and it focuses on Apple's notoriously difficult-to-crack iPhone operating systems.

Organizations hire candidates with a variety of soft skills, including strong analytical capabilities, the ability to organize challenging investigations, the capacity to document and share findings with stakeholders, and strong written and verbal communication talents.

WHAT DO DIGITAL FORENSICS EXPERTS DO?

Nowadays, virtually every legal investigation includes a digital component. Currently, digital forensics is a crucial part of most investigations, including those involving fraud, espionage, arson, theft, and wrongful death as well as civil cases including infidelity, child custody, accident reconstruction, civil disputes, and missing persons. Data security breaches are a significant concern for experts in digital forensics.

Experts in digital forensics gather all relevant evidence while conducting thorough investigations using their knowledge of all aspects of information technology and security. The spectrum of computer hardware, software, networking configurations, and mobile systems covered by this is extensive.

With this knowledge, digital forensics professionals will attempt to retrieve lost data, look through recoverable data, and perform a comprehensive forensic study of all computers, databases, and systems. The affected parties are informed once the incident is recreated using the data that was collected. In civil or criminal cases that have advanced to the legal court stage, experts in digital forensics are routinely called upon to testify.

DIGITAL FORENSICS EXPERT JOB DESCRIPTION

The precise responsibilities of digital forensics experts will vary substantially depending on the goals of the employer and the particular case being worked on. Some tasks may include one or more of the following:

- Adhere to accepted forensic best practices for the industry while handling physical media and imaging, storing, moving, and handling electronic data.
- Locate, collect, store, and review electronic data on servers, backup media, mobile devices, laptops, desktops, and various other media by using the best forensic software.
- Retrieving hidden data, cached, file fragments, and lost user data.
- Control and monitor digital evidence.

- Recognize and record the strategies, tactics, and processes an attacker might employ to gain unauthorized access.

- Submit a statement from an expert witness

CHIEF INFORMATION SECURITY OFFICER

The organization's IT security section is managed and supervised by the chief information security officer. This is typically a mid-executive level position. Every requirement for computer, network, and data security made by their companies is normally organized, directed, and planned by CISOs. CISOs work together with management to determine the specific cybersecurity needs of a company. The role of CISO requires someone with solid knowledge in IT security architecture and strategy as well as good communication and human resource management skills. CISOs are often responsible with hiring a skilled team of security professionals.

FIVE STEPS TO BECOMING A CHIEF INFORMATION SECURITY OFFICER

1. **Self-analysis**: The management and activities of an organization's IT security division are under the control of the chief information security officer. This position usually belongs to the mid-executive level. All of their companies' requirements for computer, network, and data security are normally organized, directed, and planned by CISOs. CISOs work collaboratively with management to determine a company's specific cybersecurity needs. A strong background

in IT security architecture and strategy, as well as strong communication and human resource management skills, are required for the post of CISO, which often involves hiring a skilled team of security professionals.

2. **Education**: Due to the wide and varied responsibilities of the Chief Infosec Officer post, laying the groundwork for a future in this role can take many different forms. Unquestionably, a business administration or InfoSec undergraduate degree is a great place to start, but practically any computer- or business-related field would be suitable. For protecting people and resources, security training may be a great place to start. Of course, c-suite executives like CISOs are typically, if not always, asked to pursue more education. The best degrees for you will be master's degrees in highly specialized InfoSec disciplines, as well as Ph.D. degrees when desired or necessary.

3. **Career path**: Similar to education, there are many different professional paths that one can take to become a chief infosec officer. It would be impossible to list all the possible scenarios here. Data gives crucial insight on how to become a CISO and how the position is currently and soon will change. A candidate should also review the educational and professional experience requirements given by EC-Council in order to be qualified to take the exam for the certification of chief information security officers.

4. **Professional certifications**: A candidate may be able to advance to the position of CISO in this field with the help of numerous certifications. It's generally advisable to remember

to include any supplemental talents that might be applicable to the positions along with your certifications for each field you've worked in on a resume.

The CCISO certification is the highest award for chief information security officers. The certifications and training programs offered by organizations like OSCP (Offensive Security Certified Professional), SANS Technology Institute, ISFCE (International Society of Forensic Computer Examiners), IACIS (The International Association of Computer Investigative Specialists), CISSP (Certified Information Systems Security Professional), and (ISC)2 (International Information Systems Security) are also very helpful. Furthermore, less sophisticated certifications like CompTIA A+, which attests to technical support and operational IT skills, may be helpful. For information security managers and auditors, ISACA (Information Systems Audit and Control Association) offers the certificates Certified in the Governance of Enterprise IT (CGEIT) and Certified Information Systems Auditor.

5. **Keep current**: It's crucial to keep up with advancements in the area, as it is for the bulk of cybersecurity professional employment. Being informed on current trends is even more crucial for CISOs because they are in charge of deciding how all of a company's different InfoSec resources will be employed in the present and the future. Leaders in information security must be a part of all relevant trade associations and educational institutions.

These professional trade groups include the International Society of Forensic Computer Examiners (ISFCE) and the

Scientific Working Group on Digital Evidence (SWGDE). Another source for publications and data on specific InfoSec subjects is Search Security. Additionally, EC-Council provides essays, podcasts, and other content by other CISOs on its CISO Resources page. The Information Systems Audit and Control Association is yet another fantastic resource for learning and connecting with other professionals (ISACA). The InfoSec Institute has a wealth of information and training available for InfoSec professionals.

WHAT IS A CHIEF INFORMATION SECURITY OFFICER?

Other names for CISOs include chief security architects, corporate security officers, security managers, and information security managers. This officer-level employee may be responsible for managing all aspects of organizational security, including personnel and physical assets, for some businesses. In certain situations, the position of chief security officer may be appropriate.

A CISO is always in control of all information security operations inside a certain organization, regardless of their position. In addition to reporting directly to the CEO, chief information security officers usually hold a seat on the board of directors (chief executive officer). The general direction of the InfoSec resources under their control, their distribution among the many disciplines, and the supervision of all employees in their department, and communication with all other departments within the business are all responsibilities of CISOs. CISOs commonly represent an organization's information security initiatives while speaking with outside parties. Especially in larger businesses, this typically involves communication with supervisory, regulatory, legislative, and law enforcement agencies.

CHIEF INFORMATION SECURITY OFFICERS' SKILLS AND EXPERIENCE

Some skill requirements that employers may request include the following:

- With a strong background in business management, practical skill in cybersecurity technology and strategy, and practical knowledge of information security risk management

- Deep understanding of Linux, virtualization, and networking concepts

- Proficiency with professional security standards including NIST, ISO, SANS, COBIT, and CERT;

- Knowledge of current data protection regulations, such as GDPR and local needs.

- Capable of understanding and communicating the organizational financial and commercial effect of InfoSec operations.

- Comprehensive knowledge of Secure SDLC and security automation.

Since they are at the top of the InfoSec stack, there aren't many certifications that have been approved for the position of chief information security officer. EC-Council offers the most sought-after program, referred to as Certified CISO, or CCISO.

Employers are on the lookout for soft talents like strong leadership qualities and practical expertise with strategic planning and execution. They also seek for outstanding interpersonal, written, and oral communication skills, the ability to work under pressure, adaptability, and organization.

WHAT DO CHIEF INFORMATION SECURITY OFFICERS DO?

Information security now ranks as one of the most important objectives for every organization in the twenty-first century. Giving the InfoSec operation direction, processes, and resources is the chief information security officer's responsibility. The instructions and processes must also be periodically reviewed, revised, and updated to be up to date with compliance, regulatory, and legal requirements. The CISO must be a motivational leader in addition to being an interdepartmental and cross-organizational communicator of an organization's InfoSec direction and procedures.

There are five "towers" of duty that fall under the typical CISO's purview. Each of these buildings requires a Chief Information Security Officer to have extensive expertise and experience.

- Risk management and governance (policy, legal, and compliance)
- Procurement, vendor management, financial management, and strategic planning
- Information security, compliance, and audit management controls
- Management and monitoring of security programs
- Competence for information security

These are the areas of concentration for building expertise to be competitive for a CISO position, while the relative relevance and weight of each varies from organization to organization.

CHIEF INFORMATION SECURITY OFFICERS JOB DESCRIPTION

Some or all of the following could be tasks:

- Promote security testing and assessment procedures, including but not restricted to secure continuous integration, penetration testing, and vulnerability assessments.
- Implement security automation and tooling across the whole organization.
- Identify security issues and potential threats proactively, and regularly incorporate new design systems to keep an eye out for and defend against them.
- Plan and create an information security program that will grow with the organization and be aligned with it.

- Explain to the board of directors and executive team the operational objectives, strategic direction, and financial effects of information security;
- Take the initiative in regulatory compliance projects, general information security evaluations, and external audits;
- Offer strategic risk advice and consulting for corporate IT efforts, including technical standard and control evaluation and recommendations, to facilitate interactions with external stakeholders, partners, compliance organizations, and governmental regulatory and legal bodies.
- Establish and put into practice an incident management process to quickly find, respond to, contain, and discuss a suspected or confirmed event.

PENETRATION TESTER

Penetration testing is the proactive, approved use of testing methods on an IT system to identify flaws. In order to discover operating system vulnerabilities, service and application problems, improper setups, and other flaws before an incursion that could be harmful, a penetration tester often attempts to break into computer and network systems with authorization. Penetration testers must be exceedingly skilled and frequently employ testing instruments of their own design in order to "break into" the systems under surveillance. The actions they do and vulnerabilities discovered by penetration testers must be meticulously documented.

Penetration testers are the "ethical hackers," or good people. Owners of network systems and providers of web-based applications use penetration testers, also known as assurance validators, to look for security holes that malevolent hackers might use to steal sensitive data.

Ethical hackers perform vulnerability assessments (among other tasks) for pay, effectively carrying out digital break-ins, by using their knowledge and experience.

They replicate actual cyberattacks using a range of tools and methodologies, some of which are their own inventions, and take great care to identify any weaknesses in the security protocols for networks, systems, and web-based applications.

The goal of a penetration test, or pen test for short, is to investigate all potential points of entry into a computer system in order to spot security flaws BEFORE actual hackers can do so. Pen testers frequently work on extremely secret and time-sensitive projects as a result, thus integrity and maintaining composure under pressure are essential skills.

Both the capacity for quick thought and the discipline to monitor, document, and report on actions are necessary for penetration testing.

SIX STEPS TO BECOMING A PENETRATION TESTER

1. **Self-analysis**: Utilizing penetration testing is not recommended for everyone. Excellent problem-solving

skills, persistence, attention to detail, and a desire to keep up with the most recent advances in the sector are requirements. Ethical hackers need to have a lot of each of these qualities in order to succeed. Therefore, make an honest assessment of oneself before deciding whether a position in pen testing is appropriate.

2. **Education**: Businesses used to routinely employ real-world hackers to entice employees to join the "light side" and work for the good guys. However, a college degree has almost become a prerequisite for penetration testers in recent years. Undergraduate degrees in every area of cybersecurity provide useful entrance points into the profession.

3. **Career path**: There are various ways a potential pen tester can enter the cybersecurity industry. Starting in security administration, network administration, network engineering, system administration, or web-based application programming with a constant emphasis on the security aspects of each profession will provide a strong basis for pen testing.

4. **Professional certifications**: Employers love to see that assurance validators have a variety of professional credentials on their CV, especially for more senior roles. For employment involving penetration testing, certain firms now provide highly regarded credentials.

5. **Honing the craft**: In any profession, it's a good idea to establish yourself as an expert in a particular field, but as a penetration tester there are many methods to stand

out from the crowd. By participating and earning respect in cybersecurity-related activities like bug bounty programs, acquiring open-source intelligence (OSINT), and developing custom attack programs, pen testers can get recognition among their peers.

6. **Keep current**: As is the case with the majority of career tracks in cybersecurity, it's critical to stay current with advances in the industry. Keeping one's abilities and information current with all of the most recent advancements in programming and network security, continuously changing hacking techniques and security standards, widely used exploits, and everything else taking place in the cybersecurity industry.

WHAT IS A PENETRATION TESTER?

Pentesters and ethical hackers are the private detectives of the information security sector. The objective is to spot threats before any potential invasive operators, as is the case with many PI operations, have a chance to carry out their plans.

One of the fundamental truths about human nature in general and about digital information systems in particular is that dishonest people will always look for ways to exploit weaknesses. Pen testers investigate potential security holes in web-based applications, wired and wireless network systems, and other systems, and they assist in identifying and resolving them.

The proactive actions of ethical hackers and the initiatives of real-world hackers are in a constant arms war. In terms of knowledge, skills, and techniques, both sides always strive to outperform one another.

Pen testers use an aggressive form of protection. The goal is to give the maximum level of information security while simultaneously aiding in the closure of the gap by offensively attacking computer systems in the same manner that a real-world hacker would. Systems will therefore be attacked, necessitating the protection of information.

PENETRATION TESTER SKILLS AND EXPERIENCE

Employer expectations for new employees will vary significantly in the penetration testing field, as they will in all cybersecurity disciplines, depending on the precise responsibilities of each position and the level of the function. Associate or junior penetration testers, mid-level penetration testers, and senior or lead penetration testers denote successively rising experience levels and responsibilities in the field of penetration testing.

Some occupations still only require the demonstration of relevant skills and an acceptable level of cybersecurity knowledge. Businesses are, however, increasingly seeking candidates with bachelor's degrees in computer science or a closely connected discipline, such information security. Some higher-level professions require a master's degree.

Careers in penetration testing are usually paved with professional experience in network engineering or administration, security administration, vulnerability assessment, security testing, and software development and coding.

Examples of skill requirements that employers may notice include the following:

Understanding of specific programming languages, such as:

- Python
- Powershell
- Golang
- Bash

Understanding of network operating systems, Windows, Linux, and macOS, communications protocols, firewalls, IPS/IDS systems, virtual environments, and data encryption for mobile devices running iOS and Android.

Knowledge of common application security and pen testing technologies, such as:

- Kali
- Metasploit
- Burpsuite
- Wireshark
- Web Inspect
- Network Mapper (NMAP)
- Nessus, and others

Professional qualifications from institutions like the EC-Council, OSCP (Offensive Security Certified Professional), SANS Technology Institute, IEEE (Institute for Electrical and Electronic Engineers), and GIAC are widely sought after by employers (Global Information Assurance Certification).

Employers seek applicants with a wide range of soft skills and background, including excellent communication talents, the capacity to work independently and creatively, involvement in bug bounty programs and open source projects, and familiarity with the OWASP Top 10 Vulnerabilities.

WHAT DO PENETRATION TESTERS DO?

Pen testers typically do threat modeling, security evaluation, and ethical attacks on systems, networks, and web-based applications. Any or all of the following are significant assurance validation activities:

- Provide subject-matter expertise with a focus on testing organizational defenses and aggressive security activities.
- Evaluate a variety of technologies and implementations using both automated tools and manual techniques.
- Gather and analyze OSINT (Open Source Intelligence) in order to search for information releases.
- Develop a framework, resources, and scripts to enhance testing practices.

- Help define the potential engagements' scope by leading them from the planning stage through implementation and correction.
- Perform physical penetration tests as well as social engineering exercises.
- Scan both wired and wireless networks for security holes.
- Examine assessment data to draw conclusions and develop a thorough analytical view of the system in its operating environment.
- Discover both the technical and non-technical discoveries' underlying causes.
- Distribute a report on the assessment that summarizes the results and offers potential defenses.
- Record and summarize any findings that come up in multiple assessments.
- After the assessments are complete, provide the methods, findings, and analysis.
- Technically assist ISOs in revising assessment results.
- Provide technical support for network exploitation and evasion techniques to aid in careful incident handling and forensic analysis of compromised computers.

PENETRATION TESTER JOB DESCRIPTION

The scope of penetration/ethical hacking work vary widely depending on the employer and level of skill. The mentioned responsibilities for senior-level employment can be used to determine the ideal dream job for all ethical hackers. The job description that follows can give you some inspiration.

- Test a range of technologies, including network infrastructure, online applications, wireless and mobile deployments, and security measures.
- Direct network and application penetration tests to identify security risks and vulnerabilities, with a system and enterprise focus.
- OSCP, GPEN, or GXPN certifications are preferred.
- In addition to automatic tool validation, carry out manual technical testing. Technological debriefings on testing processes and outcomes should be planned, executed, documented, and overseen.
- Execute covert Red Team Cyber operations to mimic enemy tactics and work closely with a Purple Team to test the exploits necessary to develop detections.
- Effectively communicate findings and corrective actions to all parties involved, including technical staff and executive leadership.

Information security is crucial for businesses that handle state secrets, such as national security agencies and military suppliers. This is a true job description for a senior pen test position that was issued by a prominent US military equipment company.

- Notifies important parties, such as senior leadership, of the executive summary and conclusions.

- Possess the ability to create original exploit code, avoid detection by antivirus programs, and mimic adversarial attacks.

- Conducts penetration tests and vulnerability analyses on operating system, network, and other applications, including web-based ones.
- Analyzes the efficacy of each security measure and vulnerability on the client's system.
- Conducts research and maintains current understanding of tools, tactics, defenses, and fashions in data hiding, network security, and encryption.
- Helps clients identify and mitigate security vulnerabilities.
- Boost incident response teams' capacity for reporting and other tasks.
- Develop and convey the most recent ethical hacking and vulnerability analysis approaches to junior and mid-level staff.

CRYPTANALYST

The term "cryptography" is said to have its roots in the Greek words "krypto," which means "hidden," and "graphene," which means "writing." The earliest known uses of encryption are believed to have existed at least 2,500 years ago, and some people even believe that 4,000-year-old hieroglyphics contain examples of it.

Even a century ago, the methods used were vastly different from how encryption is used now by several orders of magnitude. Today, science is employed in conjunction with advanced methods to safeguard much more complicated data.

We urge everybody who is fascinated by cryptography to find out more about its interesting past. An adequate history from antiquity to the internet era is provided in David Kahn's 1996 book The Codebreakers. The Codes and Ciphers Heritage Trust is an organization that focuses on the development of cryptography.

In the twenty-first century, cryptography combines mathematics, computer science, and engineering to design, test, and evaluate methods for safeguarding sensitive digital information.

Cryptologists must be experts in all three areas and have a thorough understanding of the most modern encryption techniques in order to decipher the codes. They are the codebreakers of the present.

CRYPTANALYST VS. CRYPTOGRAPHER

Despite the fact that the terms "cryptographer" and "cryptanalyst" are frequently used interchangeably, there is a major difference in the cryptography field.

Technically speaking, cryptanalysts decipher the codes that cryptographers produce. Those in "cryptographer" positions are usually tasked with both making and deciphering codes. Sometimes the line separating the two professions is blurred or even crossed. The distinction is useful, though, as it highlights the two distinct kinds of employers who frequently use their services.

Almost every company that wants to take data security to the next level can engage a cryptographer. Cryptographers don't just prevent hackers from accessing a company's networks and systems—they also prevent hackers who breach those systems and gain data from using or comprehending that data. They "create" or "produce" the encryption codes to protect sensitive data.

On the other hand, cryptanalysts are frequently engaged by law enforcement and intelligence organizations to decipher encryption keys used by criminals and bad actors in government. The FBI, NSA, DHS, and CIA all employ cryptanalysts to sift through data transported around the globe by known or suspected criminal organizations. Cryptanalysts need to be familiar with the most modern techniques and codes employed by cryptographers. By combing through bits of data and computer code, cryptologists "break" these codes in order to recover the cipher keys and the original data.

FOUR STEPS TO BECOMING A CRYPTOANALYST

1. Education: It's usually a good idea to get as much education as you can as soon as you can. There are a few locations outside of colleges where one can receive introductory and intermediate cryptography training. For instance, the website of InfoSec Institute provides a brief overview of cryptography. The university majors that are most suited for careers in cryptography are mathematics, computer science, computer engineering, and computer programming. When possible, courses should focus on a variety of cybersecurity-related topics. After a few years of professional experience, consider getting a master's degree because employers occasionally require graduate degrees from applicants for positions as cryptographers. Additionally, a lot of businesses will want a Ph.D.

2. Certifications/training: Although it was the first information security technique employed by humans, cryptography has few credentials.

3. Career path: A particularly specific area of study is cryptography. The ultimate objective is to ensure data security, even though it is occasionally referred to as cybersecurity rather than a field of mathematics or computer science. There are some prospects for exceptional college graduates, even if it typically takes several years of professional experience to break into the roles of cryptographer or cryptanalyst due to the technical demands of the professions. A career in cryptography also provides a wealth of opportunities outside the field of cybersecurity. But because cryptanalysts are already more technically skilled than the majority of other cybersecurity-related specializations, lateral options may be limited. Those cryptanalysts who invest in a master's or perhaps a doctoral degree will see a large increase in their professional value.

In addition to allowing one to advance in the field of cryptography, advanced degrees will also open up additional career choices, such as security consultant, college professor, research cryptology scientist, and information security systems engineer.

4. Staying current: Maintaining current knowledge, skills, and technology is essential for success in almost every aspect of cybersecurity. Because of how quickly information security is changing, specialists who are out of current may soon go extinct. Getting involved with trade associations is a great way to keep updated. These organizations frequently provide some of the best research currently accessible along with several possibilities for networking with other specialists. For cryptanalysts, it is a blessing that there are numerous trade groups available.

- International Association of Cryptologic Research (IACR)
- International Financial Cryptography Association (IFCA)
- American Crypto Association-ACA

WHAT IS A CRYPTANALYST?

To be able to interpret encrypted data, cryptologists must be familiar with and comprehend the systems and networks they are working with. They also need to be very knowledgeable about the programming languages and encryption techniques used to encrypt the data. To decode the data and unravel the cipher key used, they must also be able to search code and data piece by piece. The three most obvious applications for cryptanalysis are law enforcement, espionage, and military cybersecurity operations. The expertise of persons working to protect sensitive data, particularly cryptographers, and these advances in technology require the cryptanalyst to continuously and quickly adapt.

CRYPTANALYST SKILLS AND EXPERIENCE

Many times, applicants seeking cryptanalyst roles must have years of experience in a related field, such high-level mathematics or computer programming. Some exceptional college grads might be able to enter the field right immediately. Within federal agencies like the FBI and NSA, there are self-contained training programs for cryptanalysts that progress individuals from total beginners to experts, frequently in around three years. The FBI and NSA recruiting films provide a fantastic summary of the position and how these skills are applied in law enforcement. It is apparent that cryptanalysis is a very sophisticated, tough, and technical talent given that full instruction requires three years.

Cryptologists work with sensitive information by nature. As a result, before hiring a candidate, many organizations would probably demand that they have a current security clearance or that they are prepared to submit to a security investigation that may include a polygraph test.

These are some more likely requirements for recruiting new cryptanalysts.

- In-depth understanding of multiple programming languages, such as C++, C, Java, and Python
- Advanced mathematical skills

- Broad knowledge of computer sciences, particularly network and systems analysis
- Familiarity with homomorphic encryption and other widely used encryption methods
- Evaluation of algorithm resource needs

Frequently sought-after soft skills include:

- Strong oral and written communication abilities
- Self-motivation
- Inventiveness
- Passion and drive

WHAT DO CRYPTANALYSTS DO?

Cybersecurity as a whole is a multi-pronged strategy to thwart outside entities from accessing, gathering, and using critical digital information. Cryptography is a component of the defense mechanism. Confidential or private data that has been securely encrypted prohibits its use by unauthorized parties even if network or system attacks are successful. It's a confusing, ridiculous muddle.

However, cryptographers must be at the cutting edge of technology since hackers and technologies are constantly changing. Complex mathematics, computer programming, network system software, and communication networks must all be mastered by a cryptographer.

The challenge of developing new methods for cryptographic data protection and constantly evaluating those presently in use. Cryptographic solutions must take into account both the current architecture and operating environment as well as any potential future capabilities.

CRYPTANALYST JOB DESCRIPTION

The general goal is the same, despite the fact that the topics that cryptanalysts work on for law enforcement, the military, espionage, and other government groups vary. Decipher the encryption codes to transform encrypted data back into unencrypted data.

SECURITY SYSTEMS ADMINISTRATOR

A security systems administrator's duties, which are fairly similar to those of many cybersecurity roles, include installing, managing, maintaining, and debugging computer, network, and data security systems. The primary distinction between security systems administrators and other cybersecurity specialists is that they are often in charge of the regular operation of some security systems.

The majority of career pathways feature one or more specialist jobs that serve as a springboard for new workers. In the field of cybersecurity, the role is most usually known as a security administrator; other names for it include systems administrator, network administrator, and IT security administrator. The job's title and responsibilities will vary according on the size and nature of the organization, however the majority of cybersecurity experts starts here.

Professionals come to this entry-level role, like many other occupations, with a variety of credentials. The usual preference is for degrees in computer science or cybersecurity and experience working in the information technology sector.

However, many people enter the sector with relevant experience in technical domains and educational backgrounds unrelated to the industry. A candidate with further cybersecurity training and certifications will have an edge in these entry-level positions.

However, certain firms will require a deeper understanding of many IT disciplines. Depending on the nature of the activity, different levels of experience and expertise are required.

FIVE STEPS TO BECOMING A SECURITY ADMINISTRATOR

1. **Education**: While a bachelor of science is not required in order to be a security administrator, it is often preferred. A degree in computer science or a closely related field is also frequently requested, however it is not always necessary. After earning degrees in other STEM sectors or even liberal arts disciplines like psychology or the fine arts, many cybersecurity specialists entered the field.

2. **Experience:** In almost every career, practical experience can be just as valuable as a degree. Lack of a computer science undergraduate degree can more than be made up for with practical experience in information technology environments.

3. **Show initiative:** When someone is getting ready to start a new career path, it is encouraged to seize every chance to differentiate yourself from the competition. You must have a passion for your chosen profession and take the initiative to further your knowledge and skills on your own if you want to impress any possible employers. If you attend conferences and symposiums, sign up for training courses, or even obtain professional certifications, employers can tell that you have the drive and ambition required to succeed. The core certification CompTIA A+ for IT operational and technical support skills would be a great place to start.

4. **Professional certifications**: Because the majority of applicants for security administrator roles have little to no prior expertise in cybersecurity, professional qualifications are frequently not a requirement for accepting job offers. Any qualifications a candidate might emphasize, though, would be very helpful. And after starting an InfoSec career, getting the most professional reputation and training possible can only hasten success. There are many organizations that offer beneficial certification and training programs. Among those who engage in the industry, SANS Technology Institute, GIAC, InfoSec Institute, and EC-Council are some of the most well-known names. Do not be afraid to begin pursuing other InfoSec specialties through training and certification.

5. **Open-minded attitude**: The word "entry-level" is frequently used as a catch-all when referring to job duties. This is more likely to happen if the employer's business, nonprofit, or organization is smaller. Large firms often have adequate manpower, allowing each employee to focus on just one or a

small number of specialized tasks and responsibilities. Small enterprises, meanwhile, must make due with fewer resources. Each employee must be prepared to flip between duties effortlessly and without complaining in order to do this. Be ready to complete any duty that your boss asks you to. A successful career will ultimately result from this open-mindedness.

WHAT IS A SECURITY ADMINISTRATOR?

Assuring the integrity and security of any given organization's digital information is the main duty of any position with the title "security administrator," "systems administrator," "network systems administrator," or "IT security administrator." The breadth of the task will be significantly impacted by the size and nature of the organization.

To meet all of the digital security requirements of the organization, security administrators often work together. All tasks required to stop malicious external or internal actors from accessing an organization's desktop and mobile systems, networks, Wi-Fi apps, wearable devices, digital information, hardware, and software will be delegated to a team of security administrators..

SECURITY ADMINISTRATOR SKILLS AND EXPERIENCE

A bachelor's degree in computer science, information security, or a closely related STEM discipline is often favored for admission into the cybersecurity sector, however it is not necessary. Depending on the requirements and past experiences of the various firms, several traits distinguish the finest InfoSec employees. Many people are happy with associate's degrees or non-technical undergraduate degrees. Others demand degrees in information technology. While some employers don't demand a lot of direct experience, others prefer candidates with at least five years of IT experience, and occasionally even experience in information security.

While there are many other real-world requirements, the following are some of the typical skills and experiences that most employers seek:

- Excellent oral and written communication skills
- Attention to detail
- The capacity to continuously learn and keep up with rapidly evolving technologies
- Excellent analytical and resolving skills
- Self-motivation
- IT expertise and experience.
- Multitasking ability

WHAT DO SECURITY ADMINISTRATORS DO?

An entry-level employee who makes up a security administration team within the cybersecurity section of a Fortune 500 business is most likely one of several. As a result, each administrator typically carries out a specific task, such as safeguarding the company's email server, keeping an eye on potential network threats, or keeping up with necessary security protocols. One junior security administrator will usually perform each of these duties in addition to others in smaller businesses. Security administrator teams can be compared to an all-encompassing local police force. Teams develop and deploy defenses, uphold laws, investigate protocol infractions, and assist legislators in holding attackers accountable.

SECURITY ADMINISTRATOR JOB DESCRIPTION

As a member of a corporate security team, security administrators are responsible for safeguarding information systems from attack. The following are some of the tasks that security administrators frequently complete collectively:

- Monitor your wireless networks, wearable devices, and computer systems.
- Create, implement, and maintain antivirus and system firewall software.
- Put in place and enforce network and system usage guidelines
- Create new security procedures
- Maintaining and/or implementing measures to close these vulnerabilities
- Create and prepare recovery plans for systems and networks.
- Real-time cybersecurity risks and traffic development
- Recognize network or system vulnerabilities

HOW TO BEGIN A CAREER IN CYBERSECURITY

Cybersecurity remains a major topic of discussion in the tech sector today. These topics are routinely highlighted in the news, including ransomware attacks that shut down entire hospital networks and data breaches that simultaneously affect hundreds of millions of people. Businesses are scrambling to find efficient countermeasures against cyberattacks. The successful management of cyber risk depends on having the right group of experts on board to implement an effective security strategy.

The problem is that the industry is severely lacking in talented and knowledgeable cybersecurity personnel. Now is a great time to seek a career in cybersecurity in order to meet this demand. But how would you even know where to start? Observations are as follows:

Learn about the many cybersecurity fields

When someone introduces themselves as a doctor, an interested person with knowledge of the profession may naturally ask, "What kind?" physicians of the eyes and feet Pediatrics? The list goes on and on. The same logic applies to cybersecurity.

Depending on who you ask, there are at least 15 to 20 separate cybersecurity domains and hundreds of vocations to choose from. Each requires a particular set of skills and ways of thinking. The main point is that it might be challenging to identify areas where your passions and skills may overlap without exposure and trying new things.

I suggest signing up for a brief online course that might provide you with a fundamental introduction to cybersecurity. You can look for classes using online learning resources like Udacity, Cybrary.it, Coursera, Udemy, Khan Academy, and others. If you are already enrolled there, see if your university offers cyber security courses.

In addition, it's common to classify domains into three categories:

- Management
- Technical
- Senior leadership

The management department is only focused on managing cybersecurity within the business. Despite the necessity of understanding as much as you can about technology and the technical specifics underlying cyber risk, this field is typically less technical than others. Instead of configuring systems or digging deeper into operational assistance, an alternative career path in this profession involves using business acumen, organizational management, and soft skills to programmatically manage security.

Technically speaking, you would be looking much more closely at systems, data, tools, and networks to avoid, detect, and respond to cyber-attacks. Similar to any other industry, business culture and leadership have a direct impact on the company's success, which highlights the importance of the senior leadership domain.

Pick a career development path or, better yet, mix it up

There are many methods to increase security. Like me, I know people who studied it in school and got in. I know people who used to work in nursing, biology, history, law, and other professions who are now employed in the cyber security sector. There isn't a more advantageous path. Considering that formal academic backgrounds in the fields weren't even an option a few years ago, the majority of today's leaders in cyber security lack them.

Here are a few other ways you could organize your trip in light of that. Consider many paths to a cybersecurity job.

1. The formal education path: More universities are now offering degrees in cyber security. If you choose to pursue a career in education, look at the courses that are offered by various institutions, read reviews, and choose whether you can afford and want to make the investment.

2. Alternative programs/training and if a formal degree is not an option or a goal for them, other technical programs are emerging to help people advance their careers in cyber security. There are many more, but these are only a few examples.

- EC-Council
- Department of Homeland Security

- Year Up
- Cybersecurity-related boot camp training programs

3. The self-taught route: To perform market research, use Google. A wealth of free cybersecurity education is available online. All of them were put to use when I wished to broaden my knowledge. The best hackers, for example, don't only learn hacking in a classroom. The majority of them were self-taught. For other fields as well, the same is true. You can try to educate yourself about the industry by reading online articles, setting up your lab, and other methods. Despite the fact that many firms are progressive and prioritize competency above qualifications, many of them still have rigid requirements for education and certification.

That does not imply that there is no hope left. It suggests that you must first demonstrate that you are a subject matter expert. Second, seek out progressive companies that are flexible with qualifications.

4. The certification route: No matter which of the aforementioned career paths you choose, cybersecurity certifications can help you diversify your professional background and skill set. There are many more instances, including CISM, Security+, CEH, and CISSP.

5. The hybrid route: The final option is the hybrid route. This is the course I chose, and in my opinion, it was the best choice. I was able to study as much as I could about the profession and advance more swiftly by combining formal education with self-taught learning, technical trade schools, and certifications. As a result, I was exposed to a variety of cybersecurity areas and was able to recognize the facets of the sector that I found most appealing right away. Once I found that sweet spot, I was able to excel even more since I was competent at what I was doing and enjoyed it.

Unconventional paths to experience

A big problem arises from the fact that cyber security is such a high-risk industry and that employers usually prioritize candidates with prior expertise. It's difficult since there aren't sufficient numbers of unemployed, qualified professionals to satisfy that demand.

For individuals who are just starting their careers, it means that experience speaks louder than school or qualification. I came up with a creative solution for myself by constantly having an internship or working full-time in cyber security while simultaneously learning. I was able to do this via taking part in internships, seminars, and job shadowing. As I gained experience, I also offered my services as a volunteer to non-profits and businesses who were more willing to take a chance on me. No matter what industry you are entering or what career you are switching to, these are excellent ways to start gaining experience.

DOMAINS OF CYBER SECURITY

A good cyber security posture involves coordinated activities across all of an organization's systems because the assets of an organization are made up of a range of various platforms.

As a result, cyber security encompasses the following sub-domains:

Application Security

In order to protect against a variety of threats, application security involves integrating numerous defenses into all software and services utilized by a company. To lessen the likelihood of any unwanted access to or alteration of application resources, secure application designs, secure code, strong data input validation, threat modeling, and other methods must be developed.

Identity Management and Data Security

Authorized individuals can access information systems inside an organization thanks to identity management principles, practices, and activities. The adoption of trustworthy data storage techniques that provide data security both at rest and in transit is a component of data security.

Network Security

A network's infrastructure and network are protected from illegal access, disruptions, and misuse by using both hardware and software solutions. Cybersecurity is essential since a company's assets must be safeguarded from both internal and external attacks.

Mobile Security

Mobile security refers to protecting both organizational and personal data held on mobile devices like smartphones, laptops, tablets, and other similar devices against dangers like virus, unauthorized access, device loss or theft, and so on.

Cloud Security

Cloud security involves the creation of secure cloud infrastructures and applications for businesses utilizing AWS, Google, Azure, Rackspace, and other cloud service providers. Protection from a number of dangers is made possible by effective design and environmental setup.

Disaster recovery and Business Continuity Planning (DR&BC)

DR&BC covers procedures, monitoring, alerts, and techniques that help organizations prepare for disaster recovery and operations restoration as well as for preserving the availability of mission-critical business systems during and after a disaster.

CHAPTER FOUR

CYBER SECURITY RISK ASSESSMENT

Cybersecurity risk assessments can help organizations more effectively detect, manage, and reduce all sorts of cyber risk. It is fundamental to plans for risk management and data security.

If you work in information security, whether you like it or not, you are in the risk management sector. Risk analysis is nothing new. Businesses increasingly rely on information technology and information systems to conduct business, which exposes ecosystems to fresh, significant vulnerabilities. As a result, the panorama of digital risk threat is expanding.

A cybersecurity risk assessment measures how well a company can protect its data and IT infrastructure from online threats. The goals of a cybersecurity risk assessment are to identify, rate, and prioritize hazards to information and information systems. A cybersecurity risk assessment can be used by organizations to pinpoint and rank the areas of their cybersecurity program that need improvement. Additionally, it lets businesses to deploy resources in a way that minimizes risks and effectively communicate those risks to key stakeholders.

These risk assessments should be conducted in the context of your organization's business objectives rather than using a checklist like you would for a cybersecurity audit. This enables security teams to begin implementing security controls after conducting a high-level analysis of the vulnerabilities in your network.

Regular cybersecurity assessments are an essential component of a thorough risk management strategy since the cyber threat landscape is ever-changing. The cyber hygiene of every component of your company's ecosystem, including third- and fourth-party suppliers, must be regularly monitored. To do this, you may do a cybersecurity risk assessment to identify the online dangers that affect your security posture. This enables you to deploy resources more wisely to set up safeguards for the network and make wiser decisions.

WHY PERFORM A CYBERSECURITY ASSESSMENT?

A complete cybersecurity assessment is necessary to determine whether your company is effectively equipped to defend against a range of threats. The goals of an evaluation include the detection of vulnerabilities and the closing of security holes. Additionally, it makes an effort to keep key stakeholders and board members informed about the company's cybersecurity posture so they may make more informed decisions about how security initiatives might be incorporated into routine business operations.

Your company will continuously identify potential risks or vulnerabilities as part of any proper cybersecurity risk assessment procedure and address them. Your evaluation should be a crucial component of your company's security plan. Before starting your cybersecurity risk assessment, be sure it can produce the outcomes listed below.

- Finding vulnerabilities
- Recognition of potential dangers
- Offering options for threat recovery.
- Predicting how threats will manifest

Along with safeguarding sensitive data, the following factors should also be considered when conducting a cybersecurity assessment:

Increased Awareness

A cybersecurity risk assessment can help you inform every member of your team on the many threats to your business, their likely origins, and potential effects on their specific job functions. By adopting this method of evaluation, they will learn the importance of cybersecurity and be able to add cybersecurity-related tasks to their daily to-do list. Understanding potential threats is a crucial first step in protecting your company.

Mitigate Future Risk

No company can assert that it is safe from the effects of the cyberattacks the industry is currently facing. However, being prepared for any hacks could save your company time, money, and resources. A thorough cybersecurity risk assessment can help your business lower the danger of hackers or breaches. So even if the worst case scenario doesn't happen, this test will help your company be ready for it. When your company is prepared, you can lessen the damage a successful attack might do.

Enhanced Communication

Your cybersecurity risk assessment can improve communication within your organization. Once you've planned and carried out your assessment, you'll undoubtedly notice an improvement in internal communications. This happens as a result of the need for multiple staff members, departments, and stakeholders to collaborate and offer their suggestions in order to improve the evaluation. Your personnel will then be able to alert the proper parties about any shady dealings or potential security breaches.

It's anticipated that AI and ML technology development will continue. As a result, your company needs to prepare for the possibility that related offenses will also change. To educate your workforce and protect your assets, take the time to establish and implement a cybersecurity risk assessment.

HOW DO YOU CONDUCT A CYBERSECURITY ASSESSMENT?

An efficient cybersecurity assessment may vary from company to company depending on their industry or the area legislation that apply to them, but its core elements are always the same. Keep in mind the following guidelines when conducting a cybersecurity assessment:

Assess the assessment's geographic reach

In order to determine the whole extent of the cybersecurity assessment, list all the assets that will be examined. Instead of attempting to handle every asset type at once, it can be more beneficial to begin by focusing primarily on one type at a time. Check to see if the asset type you selected interacts with any other objects, data, or resources. By doing this, you can be sure that you're obtaining a complete picture of your entire network.

Identify the value of each asset.

Choosing which assets will be included in the assessment comes before determining the value of each asset. It's important to remember that an asset's true value may exceed its acquisition price. When performing the asset assessment, your team must take into account qualitative risks associated with each asset in addition to intangible factors.

Find cybersecurity threats

The next stage of a cybersecurity assessment is finding cybersecurity risks, which enables you to calculate the likelihood of various loss scenarios and utilize that knowledge to drive future actions. Consider the asset's prospective applications, the likelihood that it will be used, and the overall impact that use might have on your firm. This is an essential step in ensuring that your business effectively complies with any cybersecurity compliance requirements imposed by your industry.

Examine the asset's value concerning the expense of prevention.

Once the worth of an asset has been determined, the cost of safeguarding it must be considered. If the cost of averting such accidents would exceed the asset's value, determine different loss scenarios to see if it would be worthwhile to pursue an alternate control or preventative technique that makes more financial sense.

Install and regularly check security measures

Once you have identified and evaluated the critical assets and vulnerabilities within your network, the following step is to construct security mechanisms that can continuously monitor the cybersecurity of your firm. By doing so, it will be ensured that the controls are continuously protecting sensitive data and serving organizational needs.

CYBER INCIDENT RESPONSE

Attacks can be located, stopped, and neutralized using incident response (IR), a set of information security guidelines and procedures. Giving an organization the ability to quickly recognize and stop attacks, reduce damage, and prevent similar attacks in the future is the goal of incident response.

STEPS TO RESPONDING TO CYBER INCIDENTS: A LIFECYCLE OF 6 PHASES

There are six steps in the incident response procedure. A cycle of these six steps is started once an event occurs. These are the steps:

1. System and procedure preparation
2. Recognition of the incidents
3. Attacker and event activity containment
4. Removal of the assailants and possibilities for re-entry
5. Recovering from events, including system restoration
6. Applying what was learned and the advice received to the upcoming cycle of planning

Preparation

During the first stage of planning, you evaluate the efficacy of current security practices and regulations. To do this, perform a risk assessment to determine the relative importance of your assets and any existing flaws. The information is used to rank the replies for various incident types. It is also used, whenever possible, to rebuild systems in order to remedy weaknesses and focus security on assets with a high priority.

You either enhance your current policies and processes at this level or, if necessary, develop new ones. One of these processes is the assignment of roles and duties during an incident, combined with a communication strategy.

Recognition of threats

Teams use the tools and methods selected during the planning phase to look for and detect any odd activity. The team members must attempt to identify the type of attack, its source, and the assailant's goals as soon as an event is found.

Any evidence acquired during identification needs to be protected and saved for a more in-depth investigation in the future. Responders are required to keep thorough records of all actions taken and evidence found. If an attacker is discovered, this can aid in a more effective prosecution.

Preparations for communication are typically started during this phase when an incidence is confirmed. These plans advise security staff, stakeholders, authorities, legal counsel, and ultimately users about the occurrence and the appropriate responses.

Containment of threats

When an incident is discovered, containment tactics are selected and implemented. It's crucial to reach this point as soon as possible in order to lessen the damage that is caused.

Containment is frequently finished in smaller steps:

- **Short-term containment**— Threats that exist right now are curbed. For example, the current location of an attacker on your network might be isolated. Shutting down an infected server and directing traffic to a failover is an additional choice.

- **Long-term containment**— Additional access controls are applied to unaffected systems. In the meanwhile, fresh, patched copies of systems and resources are created in preparation for the recovery step.

Elimination of threats

Both during and after containment, the entire extent of an attack becomes apparent. Once teams are aware of all impacted systems and resources, they may begin expelling intruders and wiping malware from networks. This phase continues until all traces of the attack are gone. This may require switching off systems in some cases so that recovered assets can be replaced with new copies.

Recovery and restoration

In this phase, teams put online enhanced replacement systems. While it's desirable, it's not always possible to restore systems without losing data.

In the latter case, teams must locate the most recent clean copy of the data and restore it. Because it includes monitoring systems after an incident to ensure that attackers don't return, the recovery phase typically takes a lengthy.

Feedback and refinement

During the lessons learned phase, your team evaluates the decisions made during the reaction phase. Members should talk on what worked and what didn't, and make suggestions for improvements in the future. Any unfinished paperwork should also be finished at this time.

SECURITY EVENT TYPES AND RESPONSE STRATEGIES

A security event is anything that has importance for system hardware or software, whereas an incident is an event that disrupts ordinary business activities. Security events and incidents are often defined by their severity and the risk they may cause to the firm.

If only one user is refused access to a service they have requested, for instance, this could be a hint that the system has been compromised and could result in a security event. The failure of the access, however, can also be due to a number of other circumstances. Typically, one incident doesn't have a big impact on the business.

However, if a sizable number of users are turned away, it might qualify as a security event because it points to a more serious problem, such a denial-of-service attack.

A security breach is a confirmed instance in which private, confidential, or other protected information was accessed or revealed without authorization.

A security incident, as opposed to a security breach, just reveals that the information's integrity was in danger. For example, a company that successfully thwarts a cyberattack only experienced a security event and not a security breach.

There are a number of various cybersecurity situations that could result in network intrusions in a business:

1. Attempts by unauthorized parties to access systems or data

Preventing a threat actor from using hardware or software to gain access to systems or data. Attackers won't be able to utilize this way to access confidential data, an authorized user's account, or two-factor authentication. This requires the user to provide an additional piece of identification in addition to a password. Additionally, when it is being transmitted via a system or while it is at rest, employ the proper software to encrypt important enterprise data.

2. Attack using privilege escalation

An attacker might utilize the method of privilege escalation after making an attempt to acquire unauthorized access to a network in order to try to access a higher level of privileges. Threat actors have access to privileges that are not available to regular users when privilege escalation attempts are successful.

When a threat actor takes advantage of a flaw, a configuration oversight, a coding error, or any other vulnerability in an application or system to gain more access to encrypted data, this is known as privilege escalation.

Typically, this occurs after a criminal has already entered a network by gaining access to a low-level user account and is attempting to obtain higher-level privileges, i.e., full access to an enterprise's IT system, in order to either study the system more carefully or carry out an attack.

To lessen the risk of privilege escalation, organizations should constantly evaluate and remedy security issues in their IT environments. They should follow the principle of least privilege, which holds that users should only be given access permissions that are required for them to carry out their jobs. This goes along with security monitoring. Businesses should also evaluate the risks to their sensitive data and take the necessary security measures.

3. Internal threat

This is an intentional or inadvertent risk to an organization's security or data that is frequently attributed to current or former employees, third parties, such as contractors, temporary employees, or customers.

To recognize and counter insider threats, use firewalls, antivirus software, spyware detection tools, and a strict data backup and archiving plan. Teach employees and contractors about security before granting them access to the company network. Employee monitoring software can reduce the risk of data breaches and the theft of intellectual property by identifying careless, disgruntled, or hostile insiders.

4. Phishing attack

Via a phishing assault, a perpetrator pretends to be a reliable company or individual in an email or other form of communication. The attacker uses phishing emails to disseminate malicious URLs and attachments that can steal login credentials or account information from victims. Spear phishing is a highly specialized kind of phishing assault that occurs when the attacker takes the time to thoroughly research the victim in order to launch a more powerful attack.

The first line of defense against phishing attacks is users' capacity to identify phishing communications. A gateway email filter can also reduce the amount of phishing emails that clients get by blocking a large number of mass-targeted phishing emails.

5. Malware attack

This is a general term for many types of malicious software (malware) that has been installed on a computer in an establishment. Examples of malware include Trojans, worms, ransomware, adware, spyware, and various infestations. Some malware is mistakenly loaded when a worker clicks on an advertisement, visits a website that is contaminated, or installs freeware or other software.

Infection can be detected by the quick loss of disk space, excessively slow speeds, frequent freezes or crashes, a rise in unwanted internet activity, and pop-up advertisements.

Antivirus software can detect and get rid of malware. These tools can either provide an immediate protection or detect and get rid of malware through routine system checks.

6. Denial-of-service (DoS) attack

Denial-of-service (DoS) attacks are used by threat actors to take down a single computer or an entire network and prevent it from responding to service requests. DoS attacks achieve this by flooding the victim with too much traffic or information, which results in a crash.

An organization can frequently respond to a DoS attack that crashes a server by simply rebooting the machine. Additionally, servers, routers, and firewalls can be reset to stop any fraudulent traffic. Update routers and firewalls with the newest security patches.

Furthermore, network-integrated application front-end hardware can aid in data packet analysis and screening by categorizing data as it enters the system and classifying it as significant, common, or hazardous. The hardware may also be able to prevent dangerous data.

7. Man-in-the-middle (MitM) attack

When an outsider secretly intercepts and alters messages transmitted between two parties who believe they are conversing directly to one another, the attack is known as a "man-in-the-middle." The attacker in this assault deceives both victims in order to obtain their data. A few MitM threats include session hijacking, email hijacking, and Wi-Fi eavesdropping.

MitM attacks can be prevented even if they can be hard to spot. One method is to implement a data integrity, privacy, and authentication protocol like TLS (Transport Layer Security), which gives these features between two interacting computer applications. SSH is a network protocol that gives users, particularly system administrators, a secure way to access a computer over an unsafe network.

Because it is easier for hackers to infiltrate these connections, businesses should likewise warn employees about the dangers of using free public Wi-Fi. Businesses should also tell their staff members not to believe browser warnings that connections or websites might not be reliable. Businesses should utilize VPNs to provide secure connectivity.

8. Password attack

Discovering a person's or account's password is the aim of this form of attack. To do this, hackers use a variety of methods, such as password sniffers, dictionary assaults, password-cracking tools, and brute-force password guessing (trial and error).

To find a lost or forgotten password for a computer or network device, a software program known as a password breaker is utilized. This can be used by an attacker to obtain unauthorized access to resources. A dictionary attack comprises using each word in a dictionary as a password to access a server or computer that is password-protected.

To prevent password attacks, organizations should adopt multifactor authentication for user validation. The use of at least seven characters, a mix of capital and lowercase letters, numerals, and symbols, as well as at least one symbol, should be required when creating secure passwords by users. Users should regularly change their passwords and use different ones for each account. Businesses must also encrypt any passwords held in secure storage areas.

9. Web application attack

This category includes any occurrence where a web application is used as the attack's vector. This includes exploiting program-level bugs as well as disabling authentication mechanisms. One kind of web application assault is called a cross-site scripting attack. This sort of security attack involves the insertion of data, such as a malicious script, into content from websites that are typically trustworthy.

Businesses should perform code analysis early in the development process to identify vulnerabilities. Scanners for static and dynamic code can automatically check for issues. Include bot detection tools as well to prevent bots from collecting application data. Additionally, a web application firewall may monitor a network and thwart impending attacks.

10. Advanced persistent threat (APT)

APTs are laborious, targeted cyberattacks that are frequently conducted by hackers or nation-states. With this method, the attacker enters the network and stays there for some time without being seen. APTs often monitor network activity and steal data rather than hurting the network or company.

By monitoring incoming and outgoing traffic, businesses can prevent hackers from sneaking backdoors into their systems and stealing confidential data. Businesses must also build web application firewalls at the periphery of their networks to filter traffic entering their web application servers. This can help to eliminate application layer attacks, like SQL injection attacks, which are typically used during the APT penetration phase. Internal traffic can also be monitored by a network firewall.

HOW TO DETECT SECURITY INCIDENTS

Nearly every day, there are new stories about some high-profile data leak or another. But a lot more incidents get unreported because firms are unable to identify them.

Here are a few ways companies can discover security incidents:

- **Unexpected operations by privileged user account**
  Unusual activity in a privileged user account could indicate that someone is attempting to gain access to a company's network.

- **Insiders attempting to access servers and data without authorization** Many insiders may test the waters to determine exactly which systems and data they may access. Red signs include unauthorized users attempting to access servers and data, users requesting access to information unrelated to their jobs, persons logging in at ominous hours from ominous locations, or users logging in rapidly from several locations.

- **Inconsistencies in network traffic heading out** More than just network traffic is something that organizations should be worried about. Businesses should be alert for vehicles leaving their property boundaries. Insiders may send a substantial amount of emails with attachments outside the company, post massive data to personal cloud apps, or download enormous files to external storage devices like USB flash drives.

- **Transmissions to or from unidentified areas** Any traffic directed to other countries for a company that only does business there could be an indication of criminal behavior. Administrators should examine all traffic to unknown networks to ascertain its validity.

- **Excess consumption** Performance spikes on the server's hard disk or RAM could be a sign that someone is accessing those parts unlawfully.

- **Modifications to configuration** Unauthorized changes to the firewall, startup software installations, or service configurations are signs of potentially malicious activities. For recently added scheduled tasks, the same holds true.

- **Hidden data** these can be viewed as suspicious because of their file names, sizes, or locations, which imply that the data or logs may have been compromised.

- **Unexpected adjustments** password modifications, user account lockouts, and unexpected changes to group memberships are among them.

- **Odd web browsing habits** unwanted redirects, browser setting changes, or persistent pop-ups could all be examples of this.

- **Untrustworthy registry entries** this usually happens when malware attacks Windows systems. It's one of the main techniques by which malware ensures that it stays on the infected system.

CAUSES OF INCIDENT RESPONSE PROBLEMS

- Due to the lack of event context, a time-consuming manual analysis is required.
- The absence of communication channels that would have allowed analysts to easily notify and inform others about the incident
- Inefficient prioritization wastes time for security analysts.

- The inability of security teams to collaborate productively with other departments, such as operations, development, or others.
- The company's other divisions, including senior management, the legal and PR teams, clients, and shareholders, are unaware of security-related incidents.

CASES OF SECURITY-RELATED OCCURRENCES

Security professionals found the Stuxnet worm, which was meant to attack Iran's nuclear program, in 2010. One of the most sophisticated malware samples ever discovered, it is still recognized as such. The malware was developed to attack supervisory control and data acquisition systems, and it spread through infected USB devices. Although neither nation has officially admitted to being behind Stuxnet, there have been unofficial confirmations that both the United States and Israel were involved.

In October 2016, cybercriminals conducted a distributed denial-of-service attack (DDoS) against domain name system provider Dyn, interrupting web services all around the world. Another big security incident occurred. The attack had an effect on a number of websites, including the PlayStation Network, Netflix, Twitter, PayPal, and others.

A significant hack that was discovered in July 2017 exposed 14 million Verizon Communications Inc. customers' information, including phone numbers and account PINs, to the internet. According to Verizon Communications Inc., no data was taken. A researcher from security firm UpGuard first found the data on a cloud server hosted by Nice Systems, a data analytics company, a month earlier. The security firm claims that since the data wasn't password-protected, scammers could have easily grabbed it and exploited it.

WHAT IS AN INCIDENT RESPONSE PLAN (IRP)?

A documented set of instructions defining the steps to be done at each stage of an incident is known as an incident response plan (IRP). Standards for roles and responsibilities, communication techniques, and predetermined response times should all be included.

In your IRP, it's critical to define any ambiguous wording and utilize straightforward language. The terms event, alarm, and incident are commonly used interchangeably. The following guidelines for limiting their use in your plan can be useful:

- **Event**— a change to the system settings, communication, or status. Sending server queries, altering permissions, and removing data are a few examples.
- **Alert**— a warning brought on by a circumstance. Alerts can let you know when something unexpected or commonplace is happening that needs your attention. Using an unused port instead of running out of storage space is one example.

- **Incident**— a circumstance that endangers your system. As an illustration, credential theft or virus installation.

REASONS WHY YOU NEED AN INCIDENT RESPONSE PLAN

When brand reputation, financial viability, and customer confidence are at stake, an organization's capacity to identify and address security issues and incidents is essential. Regardless of how big or little the breach is, organizations need to have an incident response plan in place to lessen the likelihood that they will be the target of the most recent cyber-attack.

Incident response strategies and plans outline the following topics: the definition of a breach, the roles and responsibilities of the security team, the tools for managing a breach, the actions that must be taken to address a security incident, how the incident will be investigated and communicated, and the notification obligations following a data breach.

The following list includes the main explanations for having an incident response plan in modern times.

Protect Your Data

For both personal and professional reasons, data security is essential. Data loss can be avoided by your team by following an updated incident response plan. Data in the wrong hands could be held for ransom when a hacker uses ransomware

(WannaCry, Petya, NotPetya, etc.), or when private information is made public.

Protecting data assets during the incident response process involves a variety of tasks and responsibilities for the IR team. It is essential to perform secure backups, monitor logs and security warnings for suspicious activity, control identities and access to prevent insider threats, and apply patches carefully.

Protect Your Reputation & Customer Trust

Consumers would switch organizations 78% of the time if a data leak directly impacted them, according to IDC. The company stands the risk of losing some or all of its customers if a security breach is not swiftly fixed. After a data leak, clients won't have faith in you. By now, you're aware that it may actually be a PR disaster for firms.

Additionally, if your company is publicly traded, a publicized data breach may cause a severe decline in investor and shareholder trust. Just look at the stock prices of some of the businesses that have lately suffered from some of the worst data breaches, like Equifax, Target, Yahoo, Sony, and many others.

Protect Your Revenue

Your company is shielded from potential revenue loss by a thorough incident response plan. A data breach is estimated to cost an average of $3.6 million by the Ponemon Institute's 2017 Cost of Data Breach Study. For instance, take a look at the Home Depot data breach, which cost $62 million overall and impacted over 65 million customer credit and debit card accounts. The Target data breach, which also resulted in a 10% decline in stock price, exposed more than 100 million customer records.

Any significant data breach has a monetary cost. Even though your small to midsize firm might not be Home Depot or Target, a data breach can nonetheless have a big impact on it. In the six months following a data breach, 60% of small and medium-sized businesses fail. The cost of cleanup, forensic investigations, legal fees, and regulatory and compliance fines are also at risk when dealing with security breaches in addition to the immediate company revenue.

The sooner your firm can detect and react to a data breach or simply a security event, the less probable it is that it will significantly affect your data, customer confidence, reputation, and a potential loss in revenue. If your business doesn't currently have an incident response process in place, think about utilizing a third-party managed security services provider to create a customized strategy for it.

Reduce Downtime

One of the main advantages of having an incident response strategy is that it will significantly reduce downtime for your business. A managed service provider would develop a complete action plan for each situation and give personnel suggestions on how to tackle various issues.

Daily data backups will also be created by an IT service provider and uploaded to a distant cloud server. These backups of your data will provide your company peace of mind that it is safe and that you can access it conveniently from another location with internet access.

Remain in Compliance

Many businesses place a great focus on compliance, particularly in the legal and healthcare industries. Data security protocol violations may result in high fines and drawn-out legal proceedings. Numerous businesses simply cannot afford to disregard these strict regulations or make any short cuts. The creation of a business continuity plan and incident management, however, will help to ensure that your company complies with all rules in your particular industry. An IT service provider will also stay up to date on the most recent laws and help your business create a thorough plan for a variety of contingencies so that it always complies.

An IT support provider may develop a business continuity plan, which is the best method to prepare for any event. A managed service provider will also constantly look for ways to improve the business continuity plan so that your company is prepared for any disaster.

Today's workplaces can gain from using an IT service provider in a number of ways, including decreased downtime, increased public trust, and compliance. Although a cyber-attack or a natural disaster can occur at any time, an IT provider's responsibility is to keep your data secure and help your business create an effective incident response plan.

INCIDENT RESPONSE PLAN VS DISASTER RECOVERY PLAN

An incident response strategy is essential to any organization's security posture. In the event of a security problem, an efficient incident response strategy might be the difference between a little setback and a major disaster. Incident response plans are designed to provide a coordinated and systematic approach to incident management, from first detection to post-event rehabilitation. The three main components of incident response plans are incident prevention, incident mitigation, and incident recovery.

An incident response plan's main goal is to lessen the effects of incidents and quickly resume business as usual for the organization. Each stage has a distinct set of duties that must be fulfilled.

On the flip side, a disaster recovery plan outlines how a business will bounce back from a major tragedy. Plans for disaster recovery usually contain complex procedures and protocols and are frequently far more thorough than those for incident response. Additionally, unlike disaster recovery plans, which are frequently developed by firms before of a disaster, incident response plans are developed to be implemented in the event of an occurrence.

CHAPTER FIVE

CLOUD SECURITY ARCHITECTURE

WHAT IS CLOUD SECURITY ARCHITECTURE?

A cloud security solution's security architecture, also known as a "cloud computing security architecture" or "cloud security architecture," is composed of its platform, tools, software, infrastructure, and best practices.

A cloud security architecture offers a written and visual model to specify how to set up and secure cloud-based activities and operations. This model covers things like identity and access management, methods and controls to safeguard applications and data, ways to gain and maintain visibility into compliance, threat posture, and overall security, processes for incorporating security principles into the development and use of cloud services, policies, and governance.

The protection of data, platforms, applications, and infrastructure that function or exist within the cloud is the general focus of cloud security. Cloud security applies to all cloud computing infrastructures, including hybrid clouds, private clouds, and public clouds. Cloud security is a part of cybersecurity.

KEY ELEMENTS OF A CLOUD SECURITY ARCHITECTURE

A cloud security architecture should have the following essential elements:

- Layer-by-layer security
- Centralized Component Management
- Redundant and robust design
- Scalability and Elasticity
- The right deployment storage
- Notifications & Alerts
- Automation, Standardization, and Centralization

SHARED RESPONSIBILITY WITHIN CLOUD SECURITY ARCHITECTURES

The types of service models that a corporation uses determine the best cloud security designs. Platform as a Service (PaaS), Software as a Service (SaaS), and Infrastructure as a Service are the three service models (IaaS).

The shared responsibility principle, which asserts that the cloud service provider is responsible for the security of the equipment needed to run the cloud service, is adhered to by the majority of organizations who offer cloud services (software, computing, storage, database, networking, hardware, infrastructure, etc.).

The client is in charge of protecting any access points as well as the data and information stored in the cloud (identity and access management). The particular responsibilities will vary depending on the type of service (IaaS, SaaS, or PaaS).

Infrastructure as a Service (IaaS) Shared Responsibility

A business purchases the architecture for an IaaS from a cloud provider and frequently installs its middleware, operating systems, and applications. An excellent example of an IaaS is Azure (Microsoft). In an IaaS, the client is normally responsible for any security measures they implement or own on the infrastructure.

Software as a Service (SaaS) Shared Responsibility

A SaaS enables an organization to rent the use of cloud-based software from a vendor. Examples of SaaS include Office 365 and Salesforce. With a SaaS, the customer is typically only responsible for the security aspects of program access, such as identity management, customer network security, etc. The software provider is in charge of the security backend.

Platform as a Service (PaaS) Shared Responsibility

Instead of building or maintaining the platform infrastructure required for the applications, a corporation using a PaaS purchases a platform from a cloud provider to develop, oversee, and run applications. An example of a PaaS would be Amazon Web Services (AWS). In a PaaS, the client is responsible for the security surrounding the application's implementation, customizations, and permissions.

WHY IS CLOUD SECURITY ARCHITECTURE IMPORTANT?

Whether it is private, public, or hybrid, the cloud promises flexibility, effectiveness, and cost-effectiveness. Because they enable speedy service delivery and the capability for data-informed decision-making, which aids enterprises in adapting to market changes, these are revolutionary characteristics for any business. However, it's possible that businesses won't be able to leverage cloud resources without endangering both their data and themselves.

Cloud security architecture allows businesses to take use of all the cloud has to offer, including software as a service (SaaS), platform as a service (PaaS), and infrastructure as a service (IaaS) capabilities, while limiting exposure and vulnerability. Utilizing the cloud without a security architecture could be more harmful than helpful.

CLOUD SECURITY ARCHITECTURES BY SERVICE MODEL

IaaS Cloud Security Architecture Components

In an IaaS cloud environment, possible security architecture components include endpoint protection (EPP), a cloud access security broker (CASB), a vulnerability management system, access management, and data and network encryption.

SaaS Cloud Security Architecture Components

To facilitate visibility, access controls, and information confidentiality whether using APIs, proxies, or gateways, the SaaS security architecture should contain application security, identity, access management, and a cloud access security broker (CASB).

PaaS Cloud Security Architecture Components

Both standard solutions for cloud security architecture and rare ones, such a Cloud Workload Protection Platform, may be required for a PaaS security architecture (CWPP).

TYPES OF CLOUD SECURITY ARCHITECTURES

A cloud security architecture frequently includes the elements and best practices that are important to the categories of cloud security services that the business wants to protect. Examples include the security designs for Azure, Google's infrastructure, and the AWS cloud. Two other crucial components of a cloud security architecture are the "cloud shared responsibility model" and "zero trust architecture."

PRINCIPLES OF CLOUD SECURITY ARCHITECTURE

Any well-designed cloud security architecture should be built on the foundational components listed below:

- **Identification**— knowledge of the business environment, rules, threats, and risk management strategies (supply chain and business) that apply to your cloud environment.

- **Security Controls**— defines criteria and rules that are applied across individuals, data, and infrastructure to control the overall security posture.

- **Security by Design**— covers the automation for the control and baseline security tasks. Often standardized and reproducible for deployment across common use cases, with security standards, and for audit requirements.

- **Compliance**— by embedding industry standards and regulatory elements into the design, it ensures that standards and regulatory duties are met.

- **Perimeter Security**— any points of communication between the corporate network and the public internet are protected and secured, as is all traffic going into and out of an organization's cloud-based resources.

- **Segmentation**— divides the construction into several component pieces, which limits lateral movement in the case of a breach. There are "least privilege" concepts in it.

- **User Identity and Access Management**— Ensure knowledge, control, and visibility over each user who accesses company resources (including people, machines, and systems). Access, authorization, and protocol enforcement are all permitted.

- **Data encryption**— to lessen the impact of breaches, data is encrypted both while it is in motion and while it is being moved between internal and external cloud connection points.

- **Automation**— makes it possible to deliver security and configuration upgrades and detect threats quickly.

- **Logging and Monitoring**— by continuously monitoring (often automatically) all behavior on connected systems and cloud-based services, it ensures compliance, insight into operations, and danger awareness.

- **Visibility**— includes techniques and tools to monitor a company's numerous cloud deployments.

- **Flexible Design**— ensuring that the architecture is adaptable enough to grow and include new components and solutions without jeopardizing inherent security.

CLOUD SECURITY ARCHITECTURE THREATS

The most frequent worries and risks that affect cloud services include data breaches, malware injections, regulatory non-compliance, insider threats, credential stuffing attacks, insecure application programming interfaces (APIs), zero-day attacks, account hijacking through stolen or compromised credentials, phishing, and service disruptions caused by denial-of-service attacks or misconfigurations. In the event of a breach, guilt is governed by the shared responsibility paradigm.

Some risks and problems might also be more particular to a particular cloud service:

- **IaaS Cloud Security Threats**
  - Attacks using denial-of-service that disrupt availability
  - Injection errors
  - Invalid authentication
  - Exposure to sensitive information
  - XML external data

- Poor access management
- Errors with the security configuration
- Cross-site scripting (XSS)
- Insufficient tracking and monitoring
- Using components that have known flaws
- Information leaking due to insecure deserialization (through inadequate ACL)
- Privilege escalation caused by configuration errors
- DoS attack based on API
- Protecting low-privileged keys
- Virtual machine (VM) errors
- Illegal exploitation of data

- **PaaS Cloud Security Threats**
    - Privilege escalation for APIs
    - Issues with platform service authorization
    - Run-time engine deficiencies
    - Attacks using denial-of-service that hinder accessibility
    - Issues with access control
    - Injection mistakes
    - Deserialization with a security component
    - Using components that have known security flaws
    - Inadequate logging and monitoring
    - Unreliable authentication
    - A configuration error that escalates privileges
    - Data thievery (through inadequate ACL)
    - Cross-site scripting (XSS)
    - Difficulties with virtual machines (VMs)

- Inadequate key security for privileged access
- External entities in XML
- Security configuration errors
- API DoS attacks

- **SaaS Cloud Security Threats**
    - Hidden IT and unauthorized cloud software
    - Stolen or compromised credentials
    - Attack using stuffed credentials
    - Denial-of-service attacks that disrupt services
    - Inadequate compliance and audit supervision
    - Inadequate cloud security protocols
    - Phishing
    - Inadequate vulnerability monitoring
    - Zero-day vulnerabilities

CHAPTER SIX

CYBERSECURITY ISSUES THAT ORGANIZATIONS FACE

Cybersecurity is a major worry for today's business owners and IT leaders, and for good reason. Because hackers are aware of the regular faults that impact businesses and organizations, cybersecurity experts must constantly be on guard. Access to the internet is expanding as a result of technical improvements, which raises the possibility of cybersecurity issues for organizations.

Cyber-attacks on a business might happen at any time. Well-known businesses including Marriott, MGM Resorts, Twitter, and Magellan Health were targets of cyberattacks. Hackers don't, however, only target well-off individuals. More than one in four data breaches involved small businesses. These attacks can be expensive. A survey conducted by the U.S. Small Business Association found that 88% of small businesses think they are vulnerable to cyberattacks.

Financially, it is crucial to put an end to these attacks. There are many cybersecurity issues in the present business climate to be aware of, issues that possibly only a seasoned cybersecurity specialist can help to prevent.

SOCIAL ENGINEERING

Several hacking methods are collectively referred to as "social engineering" in this context. These tactics are designed to trick someone into divulging confidential or delicate information. Phishing scams are a common sort of attack in these cases. According to security software firm Digital Guardian, 91% of social engineering attacks are the result of phishing.

Phishing attacks use emails that seem to be from a trustworthy source, like a business, bank, or government organization. When a recipient opens a file or clicks a link in an email, they put their network at risk of infection. Employers must train employees on how to spot possible assaults and how to avoid being taken advantage of because the practice has become more sophisticated over time.

RANSOMWARE

Ransomware is another tactic used by hackers. The intention is to hold a user's data hostage until they pay a predetermined amount of money, which is typically a large quantity, in order to protect the company's data. These attacks can be launched by visiting a website that has been compromised, clicking on an online advertisement that contains malicious code, or by hackers exploiting network weaknesses, in addition to entering a system via email. The two essential elements of prevention are continuing to be alert in detecting and addressing system vulnerabilities as well as instructing staff employees to use reasonable caution when selecting which websites to browse.

CLOUD COMPUTING ISSUES

The amount of significant data that is spread across numerous data sources has grown dramatically since the early days of computing. Businesses of all stripes are more likely to experience data breaches as the number of devices used to store sensitive information grows. Cloud storage and the Internet of Things (IoT) have made new vulnerabilities visible. Organizations and corporations now need to take into account new security concerns in addition to just protecting their corporate PCs and mobile devices.

DISTRIBUTED DENIAL-OF-SERVICE (DDOS)

These attacks are distinguished by their timing. A cyber attacker floods the system with several requests for web pages and other items at once. The objective is to overwhelm systems, networks, or devices. In the end, this might expose vulnerabilities that hackers could exploit. As technology developed, this hack also became more sophisticated, making it necessary for businesses to stay current on the most recent advancements in order to protect themselves from these kinds of cybersecurity issues.

ARTIFICIAL INTELLIGENCE (AI) AND MACHINE LEARNING (ML)

Cybercriminals can employ techniques like artificial intelligence (AI) and machine learning to make their attacks more sophisticated and effective. Both are helpful weapons for criminals since they may "learn" which attack tactics work and which don't. Fortunately, skilled cybersecurity professionals can use AI and machine intelligence to prevent cyberattacks.

DATA BREACHES DUE TO REMOTE WORK

As more people choose to work from home or other locations besides the workplace, there is a bigger likelihood of cyber breaches. Unauthorized devices may connect to other networks under certain conditions.

The currently in use technology lacks the security precautions and controls provided by enterprise-level security.

Experts predict a decline in the use of virtual private networks (VPNs). After being authenticated at the perimeter when utilizing a VPN, users and/or devices typically have free access to the network. The attackers like it. Once inside, individuals are free to switch between devices for as long as they need to.

With just one misuse of VPN credentials, an attacker might get access to thousands of devices throughout an organization. Due to the theft of a vendor's or contractor's VPN credentials, which gave the attacker access to everything the vendor did, some recent large-scale breaches have been the result of this. This is no longer a useful security precaution. Such perimeter security is eliminated by migrating to a Zero Trust architecture.

Two easy additions to security measures against malevolent hackers are two-factor authentication and multifactor authentication (MFA).

CRYPTO AND BLOCKCHAIN ATTACKS

Block chain technology and cryptocurrencies are being employed in business more and more. According to a study by Allied Market Research, the global cryptocurrency market (hardware, software, platforms, and services) is projected to reach $5 billion by 2030. This digital form of trading has evolved into a refuge for cybercriminals as a result of the slow development of the infrastructure needed to protect the information associated with these assets. Those who want to use block chain in their businesses need to be very careful to make sure that these brand-new, developing markets are covered by their cybersecurity policies.

THIRD-PARTY SOFTWARE

Small businesses make a prime target for cybercriminals. One rationale is that their smaller computer networks may operate as access points to bigger targets. It is common for small firms to lack efficient security measures to prevent theft. An example of this kind of assault is the 2013 Target hack. The incident began with a cyber-attack on a small business that maintained the HVAC system for Target. In the end, this incident resulted in the theft of roughly 70 million personal records, including sensitive data, and over 40 million credit and debit card numbers.

LACK OF INFORMATION SECURITY REPRESENTATION ON THE BOARD

Even the most esoteric board members may understand the very specific policies and procedures that many businesses have for their daily operations. A businessperson, however, speaks a different language, and tragically, most board members disregard or put off these challenges.

According to an expert, even a company IT department with a good, proactive plan for information security may not get the cash and support they need since board members don't understand cyber risks.

Even the most esoteric board members may understand the very specific policies and procedures that many businesses have for their daily operations. A businessperson, however, speaks a different language, and tragically, most board members disregard or put off these challenges.

According to an expert, even a company IT department with a good, proactive plan for information security may not get the cash and support they need since board members don't understand cyber risks.

CYBERSECURITY FOR SMALL BUSINESS

Small business operators face unique challenges in many areas of their line of work. Online security is no different. From risk assessment to finding the right resources to manage that risk, many small company owners struggle to keep their companies safe online.

In many aspects of their line of work, small business owners encounter particular difficulties. Online security is no different. Numerous small business owners experience difficulty identifying their internet risk and finding the appropriate tools to control that risk.

Due to needing to adhere to a budget, small business owners struggle to remain cyber-safe. Budget restrictions force them to often make decisions in areas where they may be uninformed. Being the best plumber, consultant, or dentist in the world does not necessarily translate into the ability to navigate shark-infested cyber waters.

This manual presents strategies for safeguarding small companies against the growing number of online dangers. It provides guidance on how to assess risk, comprehend threats, identify vulnerabilities, and implement mitigation strategies.

SMALL BUSINESSES ARE ATTRACTIVE TARGETS

Small business owners figuratively carry a target on their backs. At least, it may be how cyber threat actors see it.

According to the Small Business Administration (SBA), small businesses make up 99.7% of employer enterprises in the United States. Each of these tiny businesses has fewer than 500 employees, accounting for 49.2% of all jobs in the private sector.

The US economy depends heavily on small firms, who are also more at risk from cyberattacks. Small businesses are appealing targets because they usually lack the security infrastructure of larger companies and contain information that fraudsters can use.

Attacking a small business can frequently result in fewer beneficial outcomes than if a larger business was the target. Small businesses, however, could be viewed by bad actors as "easy pickings" because of the associated lack of security measures.

However, there are situations when a small business is considered a crucial component of the attack vector on a large corporation. Every type of huge corporation works with suppliers who are small businesses. The SBA promotes collaboration between large and small suppliers. Cybercriminals have found that launching an attack on a large corporation through one of their small business partners can be a lucrative strategy.

According to a recent SBA survey, 88% of small business owners thought their organization was vulnerable to a cyber-attack. Many firms, however, lack the resources for professional IT solutions, have little time to devote to cybersecurity, or don't know where to begin.

HOW TO EVALUATE CYBER RISK

Before deciding how to strengthen their cybersecurity posture, small business owners must have a thorough awareness of their cyber risk.

Understanding this risk will help to direct the execution of security initiatives, process changes, and the justification of security-related expenditures. Selecting a security measure is nothing more than a guessing game without an understanding of risk.

There are several methods to describe risk, but they all require an understanding of threats, weaknesses, and criticality or effect.

The threat, vulnerability, and potential impact on such an organization are multiplied to create a basic formula for calculating the cyber risk that a corporation faces.

Each of the three criteria is described in further detail below. By determining the product, risk, the small business owner will be able to make decisions based on logic rather than ones based on emotion or fear.

The risk is not a matter of numbers, despite the fact that it is described here as a mathematical formula. For illustration, suppose a small business owner wants to assess the danger of hackers attempting to install ransomware on a system that houses vital data.

When a network is extremely vulnerable (perhaps because it lacks a firewall and antivirus software) and a system is vital (a loss would hurt the company's ability to continue operating), the risk is considerable. Even while the system is still crucial, a small business's exposure is negligible and its risk is low provided its perimeter defenses are robust.

Security vendors saturate the market with frequently contradictory claims about the best way to protect sensitive information or stay safe online. To be kind, the claims made by the reliable vendors are true, but their recommendations may not be suitable for small businesses.

CYBER THREATS TO SMALL BUSINESSES

Malware and social engineering are the two most common threats to small businesses. Even though hackers may conduct social engineering operations without utilizing malware, software attacks almost always include a social engineering element.

About 97 percent of cyber threats incorporate social engineering. Social engineering is the practice of using deception to coerce someone into giving over personal information, opening a link to a malicious website, or downloading a file.

Although email phishing techniques are regularly employed for this, deceit can also be carried out over the phone or through text messaging. The main objective of social engineering attempts is to obtain a victim's account login credentials. But it might also entail persuading the victim to click on a link or visit a website so the hacker can upload malware like ransomware.

However, now is a perfect time to pause and recognize that the knowledge and behavior of small businesses' owners and employees are directly related to the effectiveness of the cybersecurity mitigation strategies they may utilize. Later in this tutorial, we examine mitigation tactics.

Malware threats

Malware (malicious software) is a broad word for software that is particularly designed to harm a computer, server, client, or computer network. Malware includes things like viruses and ransomware. An employee of a small firm may be duped into downloading malware unintentionally as part of a social engineering attack.

A virus is a piece of malicious software intended to spread from computer to computer (and other connected devices). In order to give hackers access to the victim's computer system, viruses are created. They are favored by hostile actors who attack small enterprises due to their connectivity to a larger target and ability to propagate from one system to another.

It's possible that a hacker is attempting to infect the larger company with a virus through the smaller company's computer connection.

Ransomware is a particular type of malware that locks up sensitive data or prohibits a victim from using their computer until a ransom is paid. Ransomware often spreads through a phishing email's malicious link and takes advantage of unpatched software vulnerabilities.

The data or system is frequently not disclosed even after the ransom is paid. Small businesses are typically heavily dependent on critical data. A tiny business can fail if this data is lost. Ransomware is used by hackers to take advantage of this flaw.

Email threats

Phishing is a type of social engineering attack that uses email or a malicious website to download malware or collect personal information. Phishing emails give the appearance of being sent by a reputable business or a well-known individual.

These emails usually convince recipients to download attachments or click links that lead to malicious websites. After the code is executed, the PC could become infected with malware.

Many small businesses use the email services offered by the cloud to save money. These reasonably priced email services are ideal for small organizations that don't need a feature-rich email service.

Businesses that use well-known cloud-based email services are being targeted by hackers who operate Business Email Compromise (BEC) schemes, according to a recent FBI warning.

Specially designed phishing kits that imitate cloud-based email services are used to hack into enterprise email accounts and demand or misdirect money transfers to launch the scams. Between January 2014 and October 2019, the Internet Crime Complaint Center (IC3) received complaints about BEC scams involving two well-known cloud-based email services that resulted in actual losses of more than $2.1 billion.

The majority of cloud-based email platforms provide many of the security features that can prevent BEC, but many of them need to be manually configured and enabled. Users can better protect themselves from BEC by making use of the full spectrum of available defenses.

Video-teleconferencing threats

Since the COVID-19 problem, many people have been using video teleconferencing (VTC) platforms to stay in touch, and reports of VTC hijacking (also known as "Zoom-bombing") are circulating around the nation. The FBI has received multiple reports of threatening remarks and pornographic and/or abusive images disrupting sessions.

Small businesses have long relied on these technologies to support distant workers and virtual offices, despite the COVID-19 pandemic forcing many organizations and individuals to adopt video teleconferencing as their primary mode of communication.

COMMON CYBER VULNERABILITIES

A vulnerability is a weak spot that enables an attacker to gain unauthorized access to a computer system or other device and perform activities on it. Vulnerabilities could allow attackers to access private data, launch programs, obtain memory access, install malware, and more.

The most common cyber vulnerabilities for small businesses are those connected to behavior, code injection, sensitive data exposure, endpoint security, and credential management. Various cyber vulnerabilities can put firms of all sizes at risk.

A cyberattack will frequently use two or more of these related weaknesses since they are interconnected.

Behavioral vulnerabilities

As was previously stated, social engineering is present in 97% of cyber threats. Although not all human-generated vulnerabilities are the result of social engineering, this graph demonstrates that human behavior is the single most significant factor in cybersecurity. Examples of behavioral vulnerabilities (weaknesses) include the following:

- Opening potentially dangerous links in phishing emails
- Neglecting to keep systems patched and current
- Employing poor passwords

- Neglecting to take the essential safety measures to protect sensitive data
- Visiting risky websites
- In addition, downloading malicious files.

Despite widespread discussion by industry analysts, the vulnerability of end users to social engineering still presents a significant challenge for businesses. The largest risk to breaches, according to the 2019 Verizon DBIR, is end-user error. For many businesses, targeted social engineering—most frequently phishing—is the first line of defense.

Injection vulnerabilities

Injection-related attacks are occurring more frequently. Using injection vulnerabilities, online attackers can introduce malicious code into the victim's computer.

A common injection attack involves inserting malicious code through web page inputs into SQL statements. Hackers employ tools that enable users enter data into databases, shell commands, or the operating system to carry out these attacks.

Poor input validation frequently results in these mistakes. Another contributing factor is a failure to filter or sanitize user input.

Sensitive data vulnerabilities

Security professionals advocate using encryption to store PII and other crucial data. This precaution may not always ensure data security, although being useful. There are other safety precautions to consider.

Both data at rest in storage and data in transit must be protected. The data can only be transferred if the receiver can decode it. This need entails a special set of risks.

People not taking the appropriate security precautions to secure sensitive data is another area of exposure. When it comes to data security, people are typically the weakest link, whether they keep information in plain text or in the wrong place.

Even encrypted data could be the target of a ransomware assault. Access to crucial data may be restricted by ransomware software at the level of certain files or the system level on which the data is kept.

Endpoint vulnerabilities

Any laptop, desktop, smartphone, or tablet that is connected to the business network is referred to as an endpoint. Any device could serve as a malware entry point.

Depending on the number of applications on each device and whether or not each application conforms with security policy, a small firm may be exposed as a result of endpoint vulnerabilities. Due to hacked software, out-of-date operating system patches, and application vulnerabilities, a small firm may have hundreds of endpoint vulnerabilities.

Many security specialists no longer believe that traditional signature-based antiviral solutions are sufficient because many sophisticated attackers may easily get around the signatures. The most typical indicator that an attacker has bypassed the defenses is unusual activity at the endpoint.

Credential management vulnerabilities

One of the most prevalent causes of system or account penetration is improper credential management. Users utilizing the same password across several accounts, including personal accounts on corporate systems, is one of the most often exploited weaknesses for small businesses.

Many of the recent high-profile breaches have their roots in this weak habit. It is a member of the group of psychological weaknesses. Every year, countless quantities of data are breached by hackers, most often in search of usernames and passwords.

Hackers cherish this information because they may use it to create a type of malware known as credential stuffing. By employing automated tools and credentials obtained from previous breaches, criminal actors perform login attempts on several well-known websites. This activity is known as "credential stuffing."

Due to their behavioral nature, credential management vulnerabilities can be fixed without the deployment of expensive security measures. However, small business owners and personnel must practice discipline to prevent them.

CYBERSECURITY MITIGATION STRATEGIES

As stated in the basic risk equation: Threat x Vulnerability x Impact, risk can only be reduced if the threat and vulnerability components are reduced. Due to the fact that it indicates a negative effect of an attack, the impact factor rarely varies.

Mitigation techniques are the policies, procedures, and tools that a small business owner could put in place to reduce risk and resolve vulnerabilities. Although risk is rarely reduced to zero, it is theoretically feasible if a vulnerability is totally eliminated.

MITIGATING BEHAVIORAL VULNERABILITIES

In a summary, training is the most effective way to lessen behavioral shortcomings. Although this is true for businesses of all sizes, it is impossible to stress the importance of cyber training for small business owners and employees. Instead of spending money on pricey cybersecurity systems and equipment, small businesses will see the best cybersecurity outcomes from investing in training.

The most likely cause of a successful social engineering attack is the lack of security awareness training and end-user validation. Many small businesses struggle with how to educate people about social engineering attempts and how to report them.

More companies ought to routinely test their systems for phishing, use pretexting, and other social engineering methods. To help reinforce security awareness principles, there are various training programs available; if at all possible, the training should be pertinent to an employee's work responsibilities and context. It's important to keep track of users' success or failure rates during testing, as well as conduct "live fire" tests using phishing emails and other techniques. For users who don't improve, think about corrective measures that are appropriate for that organization.

MITIGATING INJECTION ATTACKS

Keeping an eye out for odd input behavior in computer systems is an effective technique to minimize injection attacks. Modern antivirus programs keep an eye out for actions that go against human input and behavioral patterns that fraudsters take advantage of. These technologies provide a more thorough evaluation of risky behavior because they provide more flexible options for protection and detection.

Small businesses would be advised to consider making an investment in security solutions that incorporate some behavioral inspection techniques. As hackers find new ways to exploit them, traditional antivirus technologies that rely on signatures are quickly becoming obsolete. Some of these more modern mitigation technologies also come with real-time reaction capabilities.

MITIGATING ATTACKS AGAINST SENSITIVE DATA

Because using encryption to protect data is not an expensive process, small businesses should follow best practices. A VPN is a common and effective method for encrypting data while it is being transmitted.

The transmitted data should still be encrypted even if access controls like usernames and passwords are ineffective. In the event that social engineering attempts to obtain system login credentials are successful, doing this will ensure that the data will still be protected.

On several levels, increasing encryption is advocated. Databases themselves as well as the physical storage where they are housed can both use cryptography. Data encryption keys should be updated often. Data and encryption keys need to be kept apart. Sensitive data audits should be routinely performed and scheduled as part of a security policy.

Many small businesses find that using encrypted flash drives is an effective method of protecting data while it is being moved. In some circumstances, physically moving the data on an encrypted disc may be the best choice if encrypted data is needed in a far-off place.

A comprehensive backup and recovery plan will help small businesses protect their data from ransomware. Database backups, end-user storage, system snapshots, and replication should all be included in this strategy (often cloud-based).

MITIGATING ENDPOINT VULNERABILITIES

The most effective and cost-effective endpoint security strategy is to establish and implement policies that call for the patching and updating of all operating systems and applications on any endpoints linked to the company network.

It is easier said than done, as the adage goes. The same smartphone is commonly used by small business owners and employees for both personal and work-related activities. Enforcing security regulations that can restrict or have an impact on the use of mixed-use devices can be challenging. Clarifying endpoint security expectations up front is crucial to avoid misunderstandings and future policy non-compliance.

Antivirus and endpoint security software providers are continually improving their offerings. Small business owners should make every effort to stay up to date with the most affordable technologies.

MITIGATING CREDENTIAL MANAGEMENT VULNERABILITIES

Most businesses stand to gain from having stringent password management. As a precaution, you might use longer passwords, more complex passwords, more frequent password changes, or a combination of these. Actually, longer passwords—even those that aren't frequently changed—are safer than shorter ones that are.

Password management tools are inexpensive and help to simplify and enforce password restrictions. These methods eliminate the need for users to try to remember a large number of passwords. To remember various passwords for every system, device, and program that a person needs access to is almost impossible.

Password management systems give small business owners the ability to change the access rights of specific employees when utilized in a group environment.

Every time a user accesses sensitive data or websites, they should use multi-factor authentication. This process can be aided by multi-factor authentication tools.

Even though researchers constantly find other significant cybersecurity vulnerabilities in the open, the issues highlighted here are some of the most frequent ones faced by small businesses globally. Look for opportunities to counter threats and weaknesses to more effectively decrease risk.

CYBERSECURITY RESOURCES FOR SMALL BUSINESS

The National Cyber Security Alliance has launched a nationwide program called CyberSecure My Business to instruct small and medium-sized businesses (SMBs) on how to be more secure and safe online (NCSA). The Federal Communications Commission offers a cybersecurity planning tool to help businesses create a plan based on their unique company needs. The Department of Homeland Security

(DHS) conducts a non-technical assessment of operational resilience and cybersecurity practices as part of its Cyber Resilience Review (CRR). Self-assessments are a choice, or you can request that DHS cybersecurity specialists do one at your location.

DHS offers free cyber hygiene vulnerability scanning for small businesses. This solution can help safeguard internet-connected computers from inappropriate setting and security flaws.

CHAPTER SEVEN

THE ROLE OF AI IN CYBER SECURITY

Cybersecurity is affected by artificial intelligence (AI), which is permeating society more and more. AI may improve cyber security in a number of ways, including by automatically spotting threats and taking necessary action, improving network performance, and helping to identify weaknesses.

Artificial intelligence is changing the cybersecurity landscape. The advantages mentioned in this article show how businesses may employ AI systems to increase the speed of their detection and response as well as their proactivity in anticipating and addressing emerging hazards.

WHAT IS ARTIFICIAL INTELLIGENCE (AI)?

Artificial intelligence is a type of intelligence displayed by robots, as opposed to the natural intelligence displayed by humans and other animals. AI programs may analyze data and draw conclusions without human input.

Artificial intelligence is developed by scrutinizing the ways that the human brain works and by examining its patterns. The creation of intelligent systems, software, or AI-powered solutions results from these threat studies.

ARTIFICIAL INTELLIGENCE FOR CYBER SECURITY

The principles of artificial intelligence (AI) are based on the Turing test. The Turing test is a method used to determine whether or not a machine can behave exactly like a person in artificial intelligence. If the answer to this question is "yes," the Turing test has been passed, and the machine is considered intelligent. AI is made up of the following three components:

- **Learning:** According to AI, learning is the process of acquiring new knowledge or skills through experience..
- **Reasoning:** the ability to draw conclusions logically from a set of premises.
- **Self-correction:** the ability to identify errors and make changes.

WHAT IS THE ROLE OF ARTIFICIAL INTELLIGENCE IN CYBER SECURITY?

The goal of AI in cyber security is to help businesses reduce the risk of vulnerabilities and improve their overall security posture. To discover patterns and trends in cyber security, AI analyzes historical data. Then, using this knowledge, new attacks are forecasted. AI-powered systems can be programmed to react to dangers automatically and deal with online threats more swiftly.

As the corporate attack surface grows and changes, it is no longer feasible to analyze and improve cyber risks and cyberattacks on a human scale. Depending on the size of your organization, handling up to several hundred billion time-varying data is required to effectively evaluate risk.

In order to assist information security teams in safeguarding sensitive data, reducing the likelihood of breaches, and bolstering their defense capabilities with more effective and productive threat detection and threat removal features, neural networks and other AI tools and techniques have developed in response to this unprecedented challenge.

USE OF MACHINE LEARNING IN CYBERSPACE

Machine learning is a subset of artificial intelligence that uses algorithms to automatically learn from experience and improve over time without explicit programming.

In terms of cyber security, it performs two main tasks:

Anomaly detection: When unusual user behavior or unexpected network activity can indicate a security issue, automatic anomaly detection using machine learning is conceivable. This is used, for example, in Crowd Strike, Dark Trace, and many more products.

Classification: Machine learning can be used to intelligently classify data, such as emails or files, into categories like spam or virus in order to deal with data more effectively.

CONUNDRUM OF AI AND CYBERSECURITY- POSSIBLE DRAWBACKS

We all strongly support the use of AI to address security issues.

Fraudulent data can be used by cybercriminals to train AI systems. As a result, they will be able to create more complex and realistic attacks. AI can also be used to automate attacks, allowing for the execution of complex operations by a single operator.

AI systems can also be fooled by so-called "adversarial examples," or inputs that have been intentionally designed to cause the system to make an incorrect categorization. For example, if a stop sign picture is slightly changed so that it can no longer be recognized as a stop sign, an autonomous vehicle may mistake it for something else, like a yield sign. This could have disastrous consequences.

As AI is employed more and more in cybersecurity, it's important to consider potential issues and how such risks could be minimized. One method to address this is to make sure AI systems can "explain" or provide a justification for their decisions. It will be simpler to ensure decisions are transparent and responsible as a result, and it will be less likely that adversarial examples will be used to manipulate the system.

AI-based cybersecurity technologies have a lot of potential to help organizations. However, it's crucial to be aware of such risks and take preventative measures to lower them.

HOW IS AI USED IN SECURITY?

AI can be applied in a number of beneficial ways to cybersecurity. Starting with the researchers or think tanks, here is a great example of how Gartner's use-case prism for cybersecurity functions. The idea of "hyper-automation" has drawn a lot of interest since Gartner's prediction. This phrase describes the additional automation that is added to next-generation AI systems in general. This requires combining AI/ML together with automation + quality assurance to make handling alerts and issue response work easier. In other words, it will let businesses scale up no-code or low-code security and improve business agility and DevOps techniques.

The following is a list of appropriate uses for security services and cloud security:

- Finding transactional fraud
- Evaluations of the web, domains, and reputation
- Improving asset inventories and dependency diagrams
- Recognizing account takeover
- Recognizing unusual system behavior
- Comparison is made of humans and machines
- Examining procedural behavior

- Risk assessment for business data
- Entitlement and access to adaptive runtime
- Incidental association
- Knowledge of potential risks
- Text-based malicious intent detection
- Visual analysis of website content
- Tasks related to security operation automation
- Security posture and risk evaluation
- Policy recommendation tool
- Malware file-based detection
- Recognition of the same individual
- Understanding proofing

Examples of how AI will facilitate the swift identification, detection, and reaction to cybersecurity risks are shown below:

AUTOMATED MALWARE DETECTION AND PREVENTION

Artificial intelligence (AI) and machine learning, by automating threat detection and responding more effectively, can keep up with cybercriminals better than traditional software-driven or manual approaches. Machine learning techniques can be used to enhance malware detection by combining various types of data from anti-malware components on the host, network, and cloud.

A previously undiscovered sample could be a novel file in malware and ransomware assault detection that helps endpoint security measures. It may or may not have a malicious feature. The same goes for malware that can avoid detection—it might not always be found.

This doesn't necessarily mean that AI will be able to stop all malware attacks. A set of mathematically arranged rules that support data attributes make up the model.

PHISHING AND SPAM DETECTION

Large amounts of data are used in deep learning to train a deep neural network, which eventually learns to classify images or carry out other tasks by itself.

Deep learning models can obtain high accuracy rates even for ill-defined assault actions. They are used to detect phishing scams, spam emails, and other inappropriate content for the workplace.

Google employed deep learning to recognize emails containing difficult-to-detect image-based content, emails with hidden content, and communications from recently created domains. This could help in the early detection of complex phishing attacks, as well as the patterns of Internet traffic linked to spamming.

FASTER AND ACCURATE ANOMALY DETECTION – SIEM AND SOAR PLATFORMS

Whether they are hazardous or innocuous, abnormalities in network traffic data can be swiftly identified by AI. Network traffic data can be utilized to identify previously undetected attacks as well as known attacks that have been modified to escape detection using machine learning techniques.

By using SIEM and SOAR solutions, organizational security architecture is strengthened. Advanced analytical methods and machine learning are used to identify the warnings, but they still need to be adjusted because false positives occasionally happen.

SOAR is the name of the engine in charge of SIEM warning cleanup and response. It is intended to assist security teams automate the response process by gathering alerts, compiling cases, and responding to SIEM's never-ending notifications.

Threat intelligence is one of its services, giving security teams more visibility into potential threats affecting not only computer systems but also IoT devices and other integrations.

SEARCHING FOR ZERO-DAY EXPLOITS

Attackers employ unpatched software defects that a vendor has not yet addressed in zero-day attacks to infect computers with malware. Recent discussions and developments in AI, though, might be helpful. Deep learning architectures can be used to find hidden or latent patterns and become more context-aware over time in order to detect zero-day vulnerabilities or behaviors. Malicious files can be identified in the source code and flagged using natural language processing. Generative adversarial networks' capacity to mimic any data distribution could be used to identify complex issues.

INCREASES THE SPEED OF DETECTION AND RESPONSE

The first step in securing your company's network is identifying hazards. It would be fantastic if you could rapidly recognize things like questionable data. Your network will be protected from long-term damage.

Integrating AI with cyber security is the most effective way to spot threats in real time and take appropriate action. Your entire system is subject to a security review by artificial intelligence. AI in the cyber sphere will spot issues before human intelligence alone does, leading to speedier and more accurate security alerts and streamlining the work of cybersecurity experts.

DETECTION OF NEW THREATS

Predictive analytics, which can be used to identify odd behavior or trending patterns of activity, is one of the most widely used uses of AI in cybersecurity. Cybercriminals want to develop new techniques for exploiting systems. AI can help detect these new dangers before they cause any damage.

REDUCE THE NUMBER OF FALSE POSITIVES

Too many false positives consume time that could be used to address real issues. However, you can reduce false positives and quickly get your employees back to work by employing AI to uncover security issues.

AI can quickly analyze a large number of events using data science to find a variety of security concerns, such as malware and the threat of risky behavior that could lead to phishing or the download of harmful code. As time goes on, these algorithms improve, learning from previous attacks to identify brand-new attack types that are now being launched. Behavior histories allow AI to recognize and react to departures from the norm by creating profiles of persons, assets, and networks.

AI systems are being trained to spot patterns, detect malware, and recognize even the smallest details of malware or ransomware attacks before they enter the system using cutting-edge algorithms.

Artificial intelligence (AI) is able to provide greater predictive intelligence by independently picking content while reading articles, news, and studies on cyber dangers. AI-based security solutions may help you prioritize threats more effectively based on what is more likely to be used to attack your systems rather than what could be used to do so, using the most recent information on global and sector-specific threats.

DETECTING BOTS

Nowadays, malicious bots make up a considerable portion of internet traffic. Bots can present a serious risk due to data fraud, fictional account creation, account takeovers using stolen passwords, and more. Manual reactions have no effect on automated threats. AI and machine learning facilitate the analysis of website traffic and the distinction between good bots, bad bots, and humans.

By looking at behavioral trends, businesses can comprehend the differences between a safe, typical user trip and a risky, unique one. In order to stay one step ahead of the malicious bots, we can use this information to understand the purpose of their web traffic.

PREDICTION OF BREACH RISK

AI systems enable the IT asset inventory, which is a comprehensive and precise catalog of all devices, users, and apps with different levels of access to various systems. By taking into account your asset inventory and threat exposure (as stated above), AI-based solutions can now forecast how and where you're most likely to be hacked, allowing you to plan and allocate resources to the most vulnerable regions.

SECURING AUTHENTICATION

The majority of websites have a user account function that necessitates logging in order to access services or make transactions. Some websites' contact forms demand that users enter sensitive information. As a company, you must add a layer of security because maintaining such a site necessitates handling private data. The additional security layer ensures the security of your network users while they are utilizing it.

Every time a user wishes to log into their account, AI secures authentication. AI use a range of methods for identification, including facial recognition, CAPTCHAs, and fingerprint scanners. Collecting data on these traits can help determine whether or not a log-in attempt is valid.

Hackers use credential stuffing and brute force attacks to gain access to corporate networks. Once an attacker gains access to a user account, your entire network may be at danger.

CHAPTER EIGHT

THE VARIOUS TECHNIQUES USED BY HACKERS

Over the past ten years, the usage of the internet to supply essential services like banking and online shopping has skyrocketed. However, this has also increased the number of malevolent attackers who attempt to access these websites illegally by using various web server hacking methods.

Although the attackers' motives can vary, they frequently aim to obtain sensitive personal information that they can then use to demand money, engage in blackmail, etc. Additionally, a well-executed website attack may result in loss of reputation and money.

I'll stick to the techniques that anyone who wants to learn ethical hacking from scratch must begin with, despite the fact that there are numerous other kinds of website hacking techniques.

Hacking is a criminal action intended to steal or gain unauthorized access to confidential information by changing its format or exploiting security flaws. In essence, the numerous strategies utilized to accomplish this sinister goal are known as hacking tactics.

A hacker can discover your personal information that you might not wish to share using easy techniques. For your own safety, being aware of these typical hacking methods, such as phishing, DDoS, clickjacking, etc.

These factors make it crucial to be aware of several hacking methods that are frequently employed to obtain your personal information without your permission. The common hacking methods listed below come with a detailed explanation:

- **Social Engineering**: Organizations, corporate bodies, and commercial enterprises are the targets of this type of attack. Hackers utilize overt deception or psychological trickery to entice unwary victims into disclosing vital and frequently secret information. The human factor is used in this hacking method.

    In order to obtain specific information they can use to exploit the website, a hostile hacker will utilize psychological ploys on a user or administrator of the website.

    A representative of the organization, for instance, calls at random and claims to be from the brand-new tech support team. They then demand individual usernames and login credentials, saying they are required for system updates. The employees willingly provide this information without realizing it, which is subsequently utilized to access and compromise the business website.

- **IoT Attacks:** People today rely extensively on the internet for a wide variety of purposes. Sadly, hackers have produced potent malware that can easily jeopardize the security of employed systems. Because most users do not care to update the factory default passwords provided, the majority of IoT devices are extremely susceptible.

Additionally, the majority of these devices transfer data without performing a security check, which encourages the spread of malware. Smart TVs, smart watches, refrigerators, air conditioners, and home pods are just a few of the gadgets and equipment that could be compromised.

- **Man in the Middle (MITM) Attack**: When data is intercepted while being sent between two or more sites, this happens. They can so listen in on conversations and examine or change data that is being transmitted, such as financial transactions.

  Particularly susceptible to this kind of assault are public Wi-Fi networks and hotspots. The answer is to guarantee that the data is encrypted from source to destination. A VPN can let you do this.

- **ARP Poisoning**: Utilizing ARP's flaws to tamper with other networked devices' MAC-to-IP mappings is known as ARP poisoning. When ARP was first developed in 1982, security was not a top priority, hence the protocol's creators did not include any techniques for authenticating ARP messages. No matter who the initial communication was meant for, every device on the network is capable of responding to an ARP request. An attacker at Computer Z may answer to Computer X's "ask" for Computer Y's MAC address, for instance, and Computer X would regard this response as legitimate. A number of attacks have been made possible by this omission. A threat actor can "poison" the ARP cache of other hosts on a local network by using readily available tools to load the ARP cache with false entries.

- **Session hijacking**: Hackers can access a target's computer or online accounts by using the Session Hijacking technique. A hacker who wants to acquire a user's passwords and personal information hijacks the user's browser session in a session hijacking attack. Both passive and active session hijacking are possible.

  There are various methods a session hijacker can take over a user's session. One popular technique is to intercept user and server communications using a packet sniffer, which enables the hacker to observe the data being delivered and received. They can then access private information or log into the account using this information.

  During an active session hijacking, the attacker seizes control of the target's active session. The attacker accomplishes this by submitting a fake request to the server that contains the session ID of the target. Because the attacker must be in an OnPath position between the target and the server (often referred to as "man-in-the-middle"), this kind of attack is more difficult to carry out.

When an attacker eavesdrops on network traffic to obtain the target's session ID, it is known as passive session hijacking. This kind of attack is simpler to carry out because all the attacker needs to access network traffic is their connection to the target's network.

Malware can also be used to hijack sessions by infecting the user's PC. The hacker now has direct access to the computer and can hijack any running sessions.

- **DNS cache poisoning**: DNS cache poisoning is the practice of inserting erroneous data into a DNS cache to cause DNS queries to produce misleading results and send people to the wrong domains. DNS spoofing is another name for DNS cache poisoning.

    In a DNS cache poisoning attack, hackers change a domain name system (DNS) to a "spoofed" DNS so that when a legitimate user visits a website, they really land at a completely other site as opposed to their intended destination. Due to the fact that fraudulent websites are frequently designed to resemble legitimate ones, most consumers are unaware that this is happening.

    There are various concerns associated with DNS poisoning for both people and businesses. One of the major dangers of DNS poisoning is that once a device has been affected by it, especially when it comes to

DNS cache poisoning, it can be very challenging to fix the problem because the device will always default to visiting the malicious site.

Additionally, DNS poisoning can be very challenging for people to identify, especially when hackers create a phony website that closely resembles the legitimate one. In these situations, consumers are likely to enter important information without recognizing the website is a phony and expose themselves and/or their businesses to considerable risk.

Viruses and malware, theft, censorship, and security blockers are some of the main risks associated with this kind of attack.

- **Drive-By Attack:** A hacker looks for unprotected, unsecured websites to attack in a drive-by manner. The hacker will upload malicious code to the pages once they have identified the website. This results in the virus entering the user's machine and giving the hacker access when they open the page.

- **Eavesdropping Attack:** Eavesdropping is another method that hackers can use to intercept data as it is being transmitted. By keeping an ear on those who share data, hackers can listen in on this data as it moves via cyberspace.

- **Attack on the Secure Sockets Layer:** A hacker tries to exploit the time lag between user commands and the point at which the website receives them in a secure sockets layer attack. Data can therefore be intercepted by the hacker as it moves between locations.

- **SQL Injection Attack:** A SQL query is taken out of the database and used to inject commands directly into the data plane. The hacker will then be granted admin rights, which they can use to get access to the database, shut it down, and steal information and login credentials.

- **Password Attack:** The term "password attack" refers to any attempt to gain a password. For instance, this could entail a phishing attempt or a brute-force attack, both of which are regularly used to access a company's network.

- **Denial or Distributed Denial of Service Attack:** One of the most damaging cyberattacks available, distributed denial of service (DDoS) aims to completely overwhelm a network or system with instructions such that it is unable to handle them all. Due to the network's failure to respond to any of these commands, it completely shuts down as a result.

- **Cross-site scripting**: A online security flaw called cross-site scripting, or XSS, enables an attacker to tamper with how users interact with a susceptible application. It enables an attacker to get around the same origin policy, which is intended to keep various websites separate from one another.

  To trick a web site into returning dangerous JavaScript to users, cross-site scripting is used. The attacker can completely impede the victim's engagement with the application when the malicious code runs inside the victim's browser.

Cross-site scripting flaws typically give an attacker the ability to pretend to be a victim user, execute any operations they are capable of performing, and access any of the user's data. The attacker may be able to fully manage all of the functionality and data of the application if the target user has privileged access within it.

Cross-site scripting attacks have the potential to capture user keystrokes, drive users to malicious websites, launch web browser-based exploits (for example, cause the browser to crash), and gather cookie information from users who are signed into websites (therefore jeopardizing the victim's account).

- **The Man-in-the-Browser attack**: Similar to a man-in-the-middle attack, a man-in-the-browser attack (MITB) uses a Trojan Horse to intercept and modify on-the-fly calls between the primary application's executable (for example, the browser) and its security mechanisms or libraries.

    Even when other authentication factors are in use, the most frequent goal of this attack is to commit financial fraud by influencing transactions of Internet Banking systems.

CHAPTER NINE

POSSIBLE INDICATIONS YOU'RE SET UP FOR A CAREER IN CYBERSECURITY

There is no denying that cyber security is a hot concern everywhere. Every time you turn on the news, it seems like there is a story about a huge data breach or a hacked organization. Because more expertise are needed to stop these attacks, you've always considered a career in cyber security. However, how can you know if a job in cyber security is the right choice for you?

Not everyone is born with the intrinsic traits that are suitable for the profession. Understanding some of the characteristics that the best cyber security specialists share will help you determine if you have what it takes to stand beside them. This list was created to help you decide if you naturally possess the necessary skills for this field of work.

PREREQUISITES FOR THINKING ABOUT A CAREER IN CYBER SECURITY

1. You were born in the era of digital technology.

It shouldn't come as a surprise that those who have grown up around computers and have a fundamental knowledge of how computers work as well as the networks to which they are connected should succeed in this field. If you have prior experience working a help desk or other entry-level positions in information technology, you may find that transitioning to a career in cyber security is simple.

2. You have a talent for spotting possible issues.

Do you typically plan ahead and take into account potential issues or strategy failures? This distrust may irritate your friends and family, but it's something that cyber security experts can use to their advantage. Having the innate ability to foresee prospective issues can help in finding vulnerabilities and planning network architecture changes because a network's defenses are only as strong as its weakest link.

3. You're grounded in reality.

The other side of being able to predict what might go wrong with any given situation or configuration is knowing the realistic and suitable course of action to take to remedy it. Despite the fact that it may seem as though having an overactive imagination would be advantageous, research shows that it actually has the opposite effect. Their advice is so absurd that no sane person would take it because they are unable to assess the threat realistically.

For instance, it is true that a stricter security policy would be more effective than one that just required staff to create 30-character passwords that needed to be updated twice a month. The effort and cooperation needed to make it happen, though, can lessen your influence when seeking to implement other, more powerful security measures.

When you make ridiculous advice, people feel security is unachievable and hopeless.

4. You pay close attention to details.

Thousands of entries in log files that need to be analyzed and configuration information from hundreds of devices are common problems that cyber security specialists must deal with. Despite the potentially vast amount of data that must be sorted through, a cyber security analyst must keep a sharp focus on accuracy.

Lack of specificity can be detrimental to both an analyst's ability to read and analyze data and to communicate exactly what needs to be done. A single error in a line of code or an incorrect instruction given to a machine could have disastrous effects.

Even the simplest mistakes can result in serious issues for cyber security specialists; one oversight could result in financial losses to businesses of hundreds or even millions of dollars.

5. You're curious

Are you curious about how things work and enjoy taking things apart to find out more? You appreciate watching shows like How It's Made, correct? An occupation in cyber security can benefit greatly from this innate curiosity.

It's important to test new software and devices and understand how they work in the current context. The security landscape is constantly evolving, therefore the IT staff needs to be aware of how different components interact with one another.

6. You like taking on new challenges.

Having a strong hunger for change is extremely advantageous for anyone working in this field. Cyber security professionals must constantly deal with new security issues and vulnerabilities, therefore you must be adaptable and eager to learn new skills on a regular basis. It can be a little difficult to not know what will happen next, but identifying and solving previously unidentified issues also brings a sense of satisfaction.

7. You're methodical

Situations and issues involving security can be exceedingly complex. A professional cyber security practitioner will employ a number of tools when evaluating data and generating conclusions; relying just on one tool can be harmful if it has unknown blind spots.

Things are not always what they seem when it comes to cyber security issues or assaults. Hackers are sly individuals who are constantly searching for ways to conceal the facts. You must carefully address issues in order to ascertain what actually happened and provide the appropriate documentation for how to prevent similar attacks in the future.

8. You're a strong communicator

Although it is usually overlooked, having the ability to articulate complex ideas coherently is a skill that is very useful in this area of work. At all levels of technical proficiency, experts agree that communication skills are essential.

Along with your professional peers, you'll also need to explain your work or results to corporate executives with less technical knowledge. If security specialists can take a highly technical concept, convert it into simple English, and add a compelling argument to the mix, they will have a better chance of getting funds and approval from those executives.

It's possible that you'll need to change how you communicate at the last minute. The speaker must be able to scan the room for gestural indications because the technical expertise of the audience is often unknown prior to a presentation.

CYBERSECURITY CERTIFICATIONS

Although there is no replacement for a traditional degree, experience and certifications are also crucial for careers in the cybersecurity sector.

A job seeker with a bachelor's or master's degree from an accredited university who also holds additional certificates may be able to obtain employment in the cybersecurity sector.

According to a Burning Glass security hiring research, candidates for around 60% of cybersecurity roles must possess at least one qualification. The following list includes some of the most well-known certifications a cybersecurity professional can obtain.

- **Certified Ethical Hacker:** The Certified Ethical Hacker accreditation is designed to teach cybersecurity personnel how to think like hackers and is only available to professionals with at least two years of experience. The most advantageous audience for obtaining this certification would be those who want to work as penetration testers.
- **Certified Information Systems Security Professionals (CISSP):** Anyone with at least five years of experience in cybersecurity is qualified to earn the CISSP certification. Throughout the course, students will learn how to identify and fix vulnerabilities in web-based systems.
- **Certified Information Systems Auditor:** For those who routinely audit, control, monitor, and analyze their company's business and IT systems, the CISA is meant to serve as a credential of expertise.
- **Network+:** With the help of this certification, students will learn the basics of networking and generally acknowledged cybersecurity best practices. Network security, network debugging, and internet infrastructure will all be covered in classes.
- **Security+:** Students learn risk management techniques, how to identify computer system vulnerabilities, and security-related cryptography concepts through the Security+ curriculum. One of the

most important cybersecurity credentials, in general, is this one. Other topics addressed in the certification program include threat analysis and hacking mitigation methods.

- **Licensed Penetration Tester (LPT)**: The LPT is one of the newest certifications available in cybersecurity. Only technicians with extensive experience in the field and a history of accomplishment under duress are given this designation. An LPT-certified technician should be able to respond to a real-time cybersecurity threat quickly and proficiently.

Although these are some of the most common certifications that cybersecurity professionals can get, there are many other options accessible.

Some employers could offer certification and training programs that can be completed on the job. This is one way a cybersecurity professional could advance in their position and learn new skills..

SECURING ENTRY-LEVEL CYBERSECURITY JOBS

Despite certain occupations requiring a master's degree in computer science or information security, it is possible to find an entry-level position in the field of cybersecurity. Experts in entry-level security may foresee handling updates, storing backups, monitoring logs, and other lower-level security challenges.

Many instructors who instruct in associate's degree programs in the subject claim that most of their students will already be hired upon graduation due to the growing demand for cybersecurity specialists.

For individuals with a background in a related field like computer science or information technology, enrolling in a cybersecurity boot camp or graduate certificate program is a growingly popular way to break into the industry.

Boot camps for cybersecurity are designed to offer in-depth instruction over the course of several weeks or months. The training and coursework may be delivered by private boot camp businesses or training providers. To close the cybersecurity skills gap, an increasing number of the nation's best universities are now offering boot camp certificates.

Reputable colleges also offer graduate certificate programs in cybersecurity. These programs are designed for advanced learners who wish to go further into a certain area of cybersecurity. Graduate certificates in cybersecurity, which frequently include a number of courses, can make job prospects seem more competitive or prepare credential holders for more specialized work within the industry.

One position one might take at the entry level is a cybersecurity analyst. According to the Bureau of Labor Statistics, professionals typically possess a bachelor's degree before securing an entry-level work as an information security analyst. In 2018, the average pay for information security analysts was $98,350, with the bottom ten percent earning less than $56,000. Some of the duties of a cyber security analyst are listed below by the Bureau of Labor Statistics:

- Produce papers outlining security lapses and the extent of the harm they caused;

- Install and use software such as firewalls and data encryption technologies to protect sensitive information.

- Check their company's networks for security holes, and if they find any, investigate the breach.

- Keep up with the most recent developments in IT security;

A MANUAL ON CYBERSECURITY CODING

As a new generation enters the high-tech field of cybersecurity, many people are lured to this fascinating career.

Because of the opportunity to lead the fight against contemporary cybercriminals and the skills gap that exists within the industry, some of the best and brightest find cybersecurity to be enticing.

The comparatively high pay in this industry also contributes to its appeal. Due to the fierce competition, newcomers must enter these cybersecurity professions with the most up-to-date technical capabilities. Industry veterans must also acquire additional education if they want to stay relevant in their careers.

In a research report published in April 2019 by the Enterprise Strategy Group (ESG) and the Information Systems Security Association (ISSA), 93% of cybersecurity professionals believe that if their organizations don't keep up with their skills, they will experience significant disadvantages from today's cyber-adversaries. It will be challenging to obtain and keep the most attractive cybersecurity professions due to a lack of knowledge.

The majority of ISSA members (63%) disagree with the statement made in the same report that their employer provides the cybersecurity team with the appropriate level of training. This is a clear indication that acquiring and maintaining crucial cybersecurity skills must be done on the individual's own schedule and price.

Computer programming is a crucial aspect of computer science. Computer science is the cornerstone of computer security.

Whether you're studying to become a SOC analyst, network engineer, malware analyst, threat intelligence specialist, network security architect, or any other cybersecurity role, your success depends on having at least a basic understanding of programming.

Knowing a programming language can help with the mystery of how a computer hack works. To figure out how an attacker successfully penetrated a system, a security expert will frequently need to search through the digital evidence left behind. To make sense of this evidence, one needs to be familiar with the language employed to create the involved weapon.

It is suggested that security professionals learn at least one object-oriented programming language. Even while studying several languages is ideal, being fluent in only one can help you comprehend many others.

There could be up to 700 different programming languages in use worldwide, with 250 of them being the most popular. Below is a list of the top 10 computer programming languages for cybersecurity professionals.

As a result, having a thorough understanding of them will provide security specialists who are proficient in one or more of these languages a substantial advantage over those who are not. These are the languages that cybercriminals use the most frequently. Using this list and the accompanying descriptions, cybersecurity professionals can determine how current their programming expertise is and set a roadmap for further professional growth.

A security expert should consider how popular a programming language is, namely among malicious actors, before deciding whether or not to invest time and resources in learning it.

Nine of the ten scripting languages that were highlighted in this guide as being extremely beneficial for cybersecurity personnel are listed in the TIOBE Index for December 2019. The TIOBE Programming Community index provides information about programming language popularity. Below, these languages are examined in relation to one another in terms of popularity.

Understanding Java

Programmers in the field of cybersecurity have a lot to gain from using Java, the programming language that programmers overall prefer. If a programmer is more interested in creating software for computers or mobile devices than in creating web applications, learning and maintaining expertise in the Java programming language is likely to boost that programmer's employment. In order to have less implementation requirements, general-purpose languages like Java were developed. The objective is to enable application developers to design once and run anywhere (WORA). Java code that has been compiled can be run on any platform that supports Java without the need to recompile it. It is one of the current most used programming languages and has a structure similar to C/C++.

Java is an essential part of the Android mobile operating system, despite past and continuing legal conflicts between Oracle, the self-described protector of Java technology, and Google (main contributor and commercial marketer of Android).

Security experts should be familiar with Java due to its widespread use. Numerous industry sources claim that Java is installed on over 95% of commercial desktops and 88% of U.S. home computers.

Due to its similarities, Java is a talent that people who are already skilled in C/C++ may easily add. A C/C++ programmer who wishes to enhance their cybersecurity resume would be prudent to study Java as well.

C/C++

One of the most essential languages for cybersecurity experts to master is C, which Dennis Ritchie first developed at Bell Labs between 1972 and 1973. C++ was created by Bjarne Stroustrup as an extension of the C programming language. The C programming language, commonly known as "C with Classes," is effectively updated by this. Numerous millions, if not billions, of devices running Windows, MacOS, or Linux are powered by the C or C++ programming languages. The two programming languages are sometimes referred to as C/C++ because C++ is an extension of C.

Due to their enduring popularity, there is a constant need for security staff who are fluent in these languages. Knowing how to use the C/C++ programming languages is essential for cybersecurity professionals because the bulk of malware is purportedly coded in these languages.

C/C++ is, in some aspects, substantially more powerful than higher-level languages like Python or Java, despite being more difficult to master. Low-level languages enable direct access to low-level infrastructures like RAM and system operations. C/C++ is intriguing to hackers due of its low-level access, making it exceedingly dangerous in their hands.

Keep in mind that novice enemies or script kids rarely use C or C++. It may take years to learn these languages. Hackers' command of C/C++ and assembly language gives them a deep understanding of how memory is managed in programs.

Understanding C/C++ is necessary to read and interpret open source code, which commonly supports low-level system applications that are crucial components of operating systems. Many black hats rely on and use open source code in their activities.

Python

Hackers and security professionals are increasingly fond of the high-level scripting language Python. It may be used to construct websites, web applications, and desktop GUI programs. Language advocates claim that due to its wide user base, it is the best choice for unskilled bad actors to adopt. The argument is that easy access to online user support will inevitably lead to the development of a variety of manipulation techniques that can be used for nefarious purposes.

Because Python is a high-level language, its power, level of detail, and exposure to hardware are not comparable to those of C/C++. The readability of the language, on the other hand, might provide a solid indication of the intended usage of Python code. This makes it advantageous for cybersecurity specialists to master this language.

A growing number of libraries allow security teams to use Python to analyze malware, create intrusion detection systems, and send TCP packets to machines without the usage of external tools. They can therefore efficiently develop programs and automate tasks.

JavaScript

Java should not be confused with JavaScript (JS), an object-oriented, high-level programming language that is just-in-time compiled. JavaScript is one of the most important internet technologies. The vast majority of websites make use of it, and the majority of online browsers come with a JavaScript engine that is especially made to operate it. JS makes it possible for websites to employ animation and be interactive.

JavaScript can be used by malicious actors to acquire user input and browser data. Cybercriminals can use cookies to monitor surfing habits or JS to follow data submitted through a web form. In order to divert users from legitimate websites, it might be used to make phony versions of reputable websites.

These security holes are growing and disseminating. Due to their tiny differences, users are finding it more difficult to discern between legitimate and counterfeit websites.

If a person has a working understanding of JavaScript and all of its applications, both advantageous and detrimental, their employability in the cybersecurity sector will rise. A person should attempt to learn and maintain their understanding of JavaScript if websites or web applications are their area of interest.

Understanding PHP

PHP is a well-known all-purpose server-side programming language that is open-source. Large-scale websites frequently employ server-side code to dynamically display content. Periodically, data is delivered to the client for display after being retrieved from a server-based database.

Perhaps the biggest benefit of server-side programming is the ability to build user-specific website content for certain users. Dynamic websites offer more pertinent material because they are based on user preferences and actions. Website speed can be increased by preserving user preferences and information. Reusing credit card information that has already been saved is one example of how to expedite future payments.

PHP is the engine of many websites, including the more than 75 million WordPress sites. Even though Facebook's version is unique, some estimates claim that PHP powers 80% of the web, including social networks like that one. Due to its advantages, PHP makes updating websites simple, which has fueled its popularity boom. PHP is more vulnerable to outside attackers due to its user-friendliness. Therefore, more than any other programming language, PHP should be studied by people who want to work in cybersecurity.

The most common hacking assaults on PHP-based websites are DDoS (Denial of Service) attacks, which seek to make a website inoperable.

Criminals may use PHP to delete all the data from a poorly constructed website. If you know how to identify and address these PHP code issues, you might potentially save an organization's whole database.

If a cybersecurity professional can only learn one language, PHP is definitely the best choice and there are other crucial determining factors, according to several cybersecurity blogs.

Learning SQL

Structured Query Language is used to manage databases and retrieve their contents (SQL). A SQL query is a request for the database to do a specific action. By entering SQL code into a web form's input box, an attacker can change or gain unauthorized access to resources thanks to a widespread security flaw known as SQL injection (SQLi). When utilized appropriately, a SQLi can reveal sensitive business data, consumer data, valuable intellectual property, and administrator credentials.

Websites are the most common targets of SQL injection attacks, which can affect any program that uses a SQL database. Common SQL databases include MySQL, Oracle, and SQL Server. Thanks to SQL injection, cybercriminals can do searches and access almost any data they want. This could lead to the loss of passwords, bank account details, social security numbers, addresses, and much more.

Security professionals need to understand SQL, its lawful uses, and how SQL injection affects websites. SQLi is one of the main threats to the security of web applications. For security defenders and pen-testers, knowing SQL will be very helpful.

Apple's Swift

Swift is a general-purpose, multi-paradigm programming language that has been created for usage with iOS, iPadOS, macOS, watchOS, tvOS, Linux, and z/OS. It is a product of Apple Inc. It was first introduced at Apple's 2014 Worldwide Developers Conference, and it was formally released in September 2019.

The interactive programming language Swift combines state-of-the-art linguistic ideas with expertise from the wider Apple engineering culture and the variety of contributions from its open-source community. SQLi poses the biggest threats to the security of web applications. For security defenders and pen-testers, knowing SQL will be very helpful.

Due to its growing popularity among programmers, both legitimate and unauthorized, and the fact that mobile devices make up the single fastest-growing attack surface, any cybersecurity professional would be wise to learn the Swift programming language. This is especially true for those who work on security and development for various Apple operating systems and devices.

Learning Ruby

Ruby is an interpreted, high-level, general-purpose computer language. Yukihiro "Matz" Matsumoto invented it in Japan in the middle of the 1990s. In general, Ruby's syntax is similar to those of Perl and Python. C was utilized as the programming language. Regular users laud its ease of use and inherent ability to support massive coding projects. Websites like Airbnb, Hulu, Kickstarter, and Github reportedly regularly use Ruby.

Ruby is interesting to new coders, which attracts new hackers.

It is marketed as being "fun to work with". Applications can be produced more quickly and with less code thanks to the high level of abstraction provided by the language, which also handles the majority of the machine's complicated details.

Using this user-friendly and simple-to-learn programming language could be a great option to improve a cybersecurity CV.

Understanding Perl

Originally developed for text manipulation, the general-purpose programming language Perl is now used for a wide range of tasks including system administration, web development, network programming, GUI building, and more. Code can be executed immediately due to the interpreted nature of the language, avoiding the need for compilation, which produces executable programs that are not portable.

The general consensus is that Perl is easy to learn. Although it is not quite as readable as Python, it borrows syntax from numerous computer languages, including C. As a result, programmers who are proficient in those languages appreciate it.

Despite being an older language and frequently positioned as a rival to Python, Perl is particularly useful for security practitioners since it was used in a wide range of legacy computer systems. Malicious actors usually target the same systems.

Lisp

In 1958, Lisp published the first description of the second-oldest high-level programming language still in use today. Only Fortran is older by a year. Because Lisp is difficult for programmers to learn, it is not widely used. However, it possesses a huge amount of power.

Although Lisp is not often recommended as a possibility for a new programmer's first language, it is a respectable alternative for an experienced programmer looking to add a powerful tool to their arsenal.

It is well knowledge that skilled adversaries create and employ sophisticated attack tools using antiquated tools like Lisp. The ability to successfully use this language can provide the defense and security tools the cyber defender needs.

PROGRAMMING FOR CYBERSECURITY IN CONCLUSION

One part of cybersecurity is knowing how to address potential vulnerabilities. There is much more at play than that. A skilled cybersecurity professional must learn to think like a hacker. If the defender is familiar with the hacker's programming tools, they will be able to anticipate both the attacker's general strategy and the specific tactics they would employ. Security will be better prepared to protect itself if it can quickly identify the adversary's tactics and anticipate his goals in doing so.

Prospective penetration testers will gain a better understanding of potential code flaws and how to exploit them by learning a programming language. Without a thorough grasp of programming, it would be difficult to identify incorrect code or conduct an efficient penetration test.

If aspiring incident responders have the abilities to analyze breaches, analyze malware, and reverse engineer attack tools, they will excel in their field.

A risk specialist who can write code will be better able to understand, apply, and solve complex software-related problems.

With so many options, how does one choose which programming language(s) to learn in order to become a cybersecurity professional or pursue a career in cybersecurity?

This guide should assist you in comprehending your options and placing them within relevant perspective. The two most crucial aspects to consider while making this choice are what language will increase the capacity to construct successful defenses and, second, what instruments the opponents are using to produce their weapons.

Which language will enable a security professional to construct effective protections will, in large part, depend on or be influenced by the needs specified by their employer. Security programming is done cooperatively. Today's cyber world is full with threats, so defensive tools need to be both clever and flexible. The bulk of security solutions are created by vendors who provide security technology to a wider industry, while large corporations occasionally create their own distinctive solutions.

Finding the language that will best equip a security professional to recognize, decipher, or counteract cyber weapons employed against their specific system requires collaboration with peers.

Security teams that are defending comparable systems, websites, or applications might be a valuable asset when attempting to predict the tools that will be used in a future attack. Knowing the language that was used to deploy that attack allows one to deduce the language that would be most beneficial to the defender.

Each specific task lying under the cybersecurity umbrella will undoubtedly benefit from having the ability to write in a range of computer languages. For instance, a software malware analyst may need to be fluent in C to assess viral code and ascertain what it does without running it. A network security architect may find Lisp's capabilities more helpful in securing the company's networks. A website security analyst could find it helpful to have a working knowledge of PHP.

Anyone looking to grow inside their present employer's business should be able to easily determine the best alternative for learning or adding a programming language. The security leaders of the organization will know which terminology will be most useful. For those looking for a career shift outside of their current employer, a search on a tech job board would likely give clear understanding of what specific programming language is required for the desired cybersecurity function.

INDEX

2

2017, 39, 160, 163

A

A+, 103, 108, 130
abilities, 48, 60, 73, 75, 78, 82, 83, 89, 90, 100, 103, 104, 106, 111, 114, 117, 125, 127, 130, 132, 135, 200, 217
ACA, 126
access, 3, 4, 6, 7, 8, 9, 11, 15, 16, 17, 19, 21, 22, 39, 53, 54, 55, 58, 71, 76, 77, 80, 92, 98, 105, 139, 140, 148, 150, 151, 152, 155, 156, 157, 158, 163, 164, 167, 169, 171, 173, 175, 176, 177, 178, 180, 187, 189, 192, 195, 197, 209, 210, 223, 224, 227
administration, 31, 107, 111, 115, 117, 133, 227, 229
Administration, 111, 183
administrator, 67, 73, 76, 77, 92, 93, 128, 129, 130, 131, 133
administrators, 128, 131, 133, 155, 158
Advanced, 90, 125, 127, 157, 208
adversary, 86, 230
agencies, 24, 25, 27, 29, 33, 112, 121, 123
agency, 87, 178
AI, 144, 179, 199, 200, 201, 202, 203, 204, 205, 206, 207, 208, 209, 210
Amazon, 58, 77, 170
analysis, 12, 36, 38, 69, 70, 71, 77, 94, 95, 102, 104, 106, 114, 120, 121, 122, 127, 154, 209, 217

analyst, 67, 80, 81, 82, 84, 101, 213, 218, 220, 232
analysts, 79, 81, 82, 83, 84, 86, 89, 159, 190, 218
analytical, 90, 104, 119, 132, 206
antivirus, 59, 69, 121, 133, 152, 154, 185, 195, 197
Apple's, 104, 227, 228
application, 3, 56, 87, 88, 89, 95, 99, 113, 115, 118, 120, 139, 151, 154, 156, 157, 170, 174, 192, 222, 227
Application security, 89
applications, 3, 21, 59, 87, 97, 113, 114, 116, 119, 120, 121, 122, 140, 155, 167, 169, 170, 176, 192, 203, 207, 222, 223, 225, 227, 229, 232
APT, 157
architect, 65, 66, 67, 68, 69, 70, 73, 76, 220, 232
architects, 65, 66, 67, 68, 69, 70, 109
architecture, 21, 40, 42, 44, 64, 67, 71, 74, 75, 78, 106, 128, 167, 168, 169, 170, 171, 172, 173, 174, 180, 206, 212
architectures, 64, 139, 207
Artificial, 179, 199, 207
assault, 12, 20, 21, 23, 52, 88, 90, 92, 133, 154, 155, 187, 194, 205, 232
assaults, 1, 3, 11, 12, 20, 21, 35, 76, 82, 85, 95, 146, 153, 155, 156, 157, 175, 177, 178, 186, 191, 205, 206, 210
Assaults, 9
assessment, 41, 67, 95, 96, 98, 112, 117, 119, 120, 141, 142, 143, 144, 145, 147, 204
assessments, 41, 85, 94, 95, 112, 120, 121, 141, 142, 198
Associate, 62
assurance, 113, 115, 119, 164, 203

231

attack, 1, 11, 12, 19, 21, 22, 23, 48, 49, 52, 57, 63, 64, 77, 85, 87, 88, 89, 94, 95, 115, 119, 144, 147, 149, 150, 152, 153, 154, 155, 156, 160, 162, 165, 175, 176, 180, 181, 184, 190, 191, 192, 193, 201, 205, 206, 208, 217, 228, 230, 231, 232
attacker, 7, 76, 88, 105, 148, 151, 153, 156, 157, 158, 179, 180, 189, 192, 210, 220, 227, 230
attackers, 1, 3, 15, 87, 133, 149, 181, 191, 192, 206, 226
Attackers, 74, 151, 180, 189
attacks, 3, 8, 9, 12, 13, 17, 19, 20, 21, 22, 48, 52, 82, 92, 93, 94, 95, 121, 127, 134, 136, 140, 146, 154, 155, 156, 157, 174, 176, 177, 178, 179, 195, 200, 201, 202, 206, 208, 214, 226, 227
audit, 31, 34, 38, 79, 111, 141, 172, 216
authentication, 16, 39, 76, 151, 155, 156, 174, 175, 181, 197, 210
authorization, 6, 7, 76, 88, 113, 158, 175, 189
Authorizations, 41
authorize, 85
authorized, 19, 113, 139, 151
automation, 110, 112, 172, 203
availability, 15, 17, 73, 140, 174, 175
awareness, 46, 47, 48, 49, 50, 51, 70, 71, 160, 173, 185, 194
AWS, 78, 79, 140, 170, 172
Azure, 140, 169, 172

B

bachelor's, 62, 66, 80, 81, 92, 99, 117, 132, 215, 218
backend, 169
backup, 17, 105, 152, 196
bad, 11, 76, 86, 88, 90, 98, 123, 184, 190, 209, 221, 224
bad guys, 76, 86, 90

banking, 10, 82
based, 2, 15, 36, 37, 39, 42, 49, 52, 63, 79, 95, 96, 113, 114, 115, 116, 119, 121, 134, 167, 169, 173, 175, 176, 185, 188, 192, 196, 198, 202, 203, 205, 208, 209, 216, 221, 225, 226
Bash, 72, 79, 103, 117
black, 85, 88, 89, 92, 99, 224
black hat, 85, 89, 92, 99
blackhat, 85, 86, 90
BLS, 81
blue team, 86
bootstraps, 99
breach, 1, 14, 16, 29, 47, 51, 55, 76, 84, 85, 92, 102, 123, 150, 160, 162, 163, 164, 173, 174, 211
breached, 72, 88, 114
breaches, 14, 25, 28, 32, 44, 51, 56, 59, 74, 76, 84, 85, 104, 134, 143, 144, 152, 163, 173, 174, 177, 180, 190, 193, 201, 219, 231
bug, 89, 115, 118, 151
Burpsuite, 118
businesses, 1, 11, 21, 24, 25, 26, 27, 28, 29, 32, 34, 35, 37, 38, 44, 47, 53, 54, 55, 56, 57, 58, 59, 68, 73, 79, 84, 88, 96, 109, 114, 117, 127, 129, 131, 137, 138, 140, 141, 152, 155, 156, 157, 163, 166, 168, 177, 179, 181, 182, 183, 184, 186, 187, 188, 190, 194,198, 202
Businesses, 24, 47, 49, 54, 56, 134, 155, 158, 209

C

C, 83, 103, 127, 222, 223, 224, 228, 229, 232
C++, 83, 127, 222, 223, 224
career, 61, 65, 66, 67, 69, 72, 81, 82, 87, 90, 92, 97, 100, 101, 106, 115, 125, 129, 130, 131, 134, 136, 139, 211, 215, 231, 232

CCISO, 108, 110
CCSP, 68
CEH, 67, 85, 91, 138
CERT, 110
certificate, 91, 218
certificates, 59, 100, 115
certification, 30, 33, 34, 38, 67, 72, 73, 81, 91, 103, 107, 108, 130, 131, 137, 138, 216, 217, 218
certifications, 25, 37, 62, 67, 74, 80, 81, 83, 84, 91, 92, 97, 99, 100, 103, 107, 108, 110, 115, 121, 129, 130, 138, 215, 218
CGEIT, 74, 108
CIA, 14, 123
CISO, 108
CISOs, 106, 107, 108, 109
CISSP, 62, 67, 74, 108, 138, 216
clients, 2, 26, 29, 73, 75, 78, 160
cloud, 2, 4, 17, 34, 35, 74, 78, 79, 140, 158, 161, 164, 167, 168, 169, 170, 171, 172, 173, 174, 176, 179, 188, 196, 203, 205
cloud computing security, 167
cloud service, 140, 168, 174
cloud-based applications, 2
COBIT, 32, 33, 37, 110
code, 8, 18, 21, 22, 34, 76, 83, 84, 92, 102, 121, 124, 126, 139, 156, 178, 188, 189, 191, 203, 207, 208, 213, 222, 223, 224, 225, 226, 227, 229, 230, 231, 232
codebreakers, 123
coding, 62, 64, 72, 76, 90, 117, 151, 228
Coding, 79
communications, 36, 41, 50, 118, 144, 153, 205
companies, 1, 10, 25, 27, 34, 73, 87, 139, 140, 163, 165, 170, 177, 181, 189, 198, 203, 218
compliance, 24, 29, 31, 32, 33, 34, 35, 37, 39, 40, 43, 44, 52, 77, 78, 111, 112, 145, 164, 165, 167, 173, 174, 176, 196

CompTIA, 67, 103, 108, 130
computer, 3, 4, 5, 6, 7, 8, 9, 11, 18, 22, 52, 55, 60, 62, 63, 65, 66, 69, 80, 81, 82, 83, 84, 85, 90, 92, 95, 99, 100, 103, 104, 106, 107, 113, 114, 116, 117, 122, 124, 126, 127, 128, 129, 130, 132, 133, 154, 155, 181, 186, 187, 189, 195, 200, 206, 216, 217, 218,220, 221, 229, 232
confidentiality, 15, 16, 73, 171
configuration, 37, 73, 77, 140, 151, 159, 173, 175, 198, 212, 213
configurations, 91, 170
configuring, 69, 76, 136
connectivity, 91, 155
consultant, 62, 67, 71, 73, 74, 86, 87, 93, 97, 98, 125, 183
Consultant, 77
consultants, 60, 71, 73, 74, 76, 77, 79, 86
Consultants, 78
control, 1, 8, 16, 38, 39, 40, 41, 42, 43, 44, 58, 89, 109, 146, 160, 172, 173, 175
corporate, 2, 19, 32, 59, 60, 85, 109, 112, 164, 173, 179, 193, 210
corporation, 1, 28, 82
corporations, 25, 26, 29, 33, 231
counter, 3, 70
countermeasures, 64, 94, 121
credentials, 20, 37, 62, 80, 91, 103, 108, 115, 118, 129, 130, 137, 153, 174, 176, 180, 193, 195, 216, 217, 227
credit cards, 10
crime, 1, 5, 9, 10, 18, 52, 100
Crime, 9, 101, 188
crimes, 9, 89, 102, 144
criminal, 6, 7, 52, 104, 105, 124, 151
Criminal, 4
criminals, 5, 11, 13, 54, 123, 180, 204, 226
cryptanalysis, 126
cryptanalyst, 123, 125, 126
cryptanalysts, 123, 125, 126, 127, 128

233

Cryptanalysts, 123
cryptocurrencies, 11
cryptocurrency, 12, 181
cryptographer, 128
cryptographers, 123, 124, 126, 128
Cryptographers, 123
cryptographic, 17, 128
cryptography, 122, 123, 124, 125, 127, 196, 216
Cryptologists, 124, 126
cryptology, 125
cyber, 2, 5, 6, 9, 10, 11, 14, 15, 19, 26, 27, 35, 44, 47, 48, 50, 52, 53, 54, 56, 57, 59, 63, 102, 134, 135, 136, 137, 138, 139, 141, 142, 162, 165, 177, 179, 181, 182, 183, 184, 186, 189, 190, 194, 198, 199, 200, 201, 204, 207, 208, 211, 212, 213, 214, 219, 220, 230, 231, 232
Cyber, 6, 8, 11, 18, 44, 46, 48, 52, 54, 57, 120, 183, 191, 198, 213, 214
cyberattack, 51, 52, 57, 58, 94, 150, 157, 189
cyberattacks, 3, 5, 17, 19, 21, 23, 31, 44, 48, 51, 52, 54, 56, 57, 87, 94, 113, 134, 143, 179, 180, 183
Cyberattacks, 56, 177
cybercrime, 4, 5, 7, 9, 10, 11, 12, 13, 28, 52, 99, 101
cyber-crime, 5
Cybercrime, 5, 9, 11
cybercrimes, 5, 7, 8, 11, 59, 99
Cybercrimes, 7
cybercriminal, 12
cybercriminals, 5, 11, 55, 58, 94, 179, 181, 188, 195, 207, 219, 221, 223
Cybercriminals, 11, 12, 160, 184, 202, 227
cybernetic, 18
cybersecurity, 1, 2, 3, 4, 18, 19, 20, 21, 24, 25, 26, 27, 28, 29, 30, 31, 32, 36, 44, 46, 47, 48, 49, 50, 51, 52, 54, 55, 56, 57, 59, 60, 62, 65, 66, 67, 68, 71, 72, 73, 75, 79, 80, 81, 82, 83, 84, 86, 87, 88, 89, 90,
91, 92, 97, 98, 99, 100, 101, 106, 108, 110, 114, 115, 117, 124, 125, 126, 127, 128, 129, 130, 132, 133, 134, 135, 136, 137, 138, 140, 141, 142, 143, 144, 145, 146, 151, 160, 177, 179, 180, 181, 184, 186, 190, 194, 198, 199, 202, 203, 204, 207, 215, 216, 217, 218, 219, 220, 221, 222, 223, 224, 225, 226, 228, 229, 230, 231, 232
Cybersecurity, 1, 3, 27, 30, 35, 36, 52, 54, 55, 56, 57, 73, 135, 137, 167, 177, 182, 218, 221, 227
cyberspace, 7, 9, 18, 22, 27, 28, 52, 177
Cyberspace, 18
cyberstalk, 6

D

dangers, 4, 20, 50, 53, 63, 64, 82, 116, 141, 143, 152, 182, 191, 200, 207
data, 1, 2, 3, 4, 7, 8, 9, 10, 11, 12, 14, 16, 17, 18, 19, 20, 21, 22, 30, 32, 39, 43, 44, 47, 51, 52, 53, 54, 55, 56, 57, 59, 71, 72, 73, 76, 79, 82, 83, 85, 87, 91, 94, 97, 98, 99, 102, 104, 105, 106, 110, 118, 121, 122, 123, 124, 125, 126, 127, 128, 134, 136, 139, 140, 141, 143, 145, 149, 151, 152, 154, 155, 156, 157, 158, 159, 160, 161, 162, 163, 164, 165, 167, 169, 170, 171, 172, 173, 174, 175, 176, 177, 178, 179, 181, 185, 187, 189, 190, 191, 192, 193, 195, 196, 199, 200, 201, 202, 204, 205, 206, 207, 208, 209, 210, 211, 213, 219, 225, 226, 227
database, 20, 22, 168, 196, 225, 226, 227
databases, 82, 102, 104, 191, 196, 227
DDoS, 13, 226

debugging, 128
decipher, 102, 123, 126, 128
defamation, 6
defense, 47, 48, 76, 79, 86, 116, 127, 154, 201, 205, 230
defensive, 65, 69, 85, 86, 93, 99, 133, 231
degree, 62, 66, 68, 77, 80, 81, 92, 99, 100, 107, 114, 117, 124, 125, 130, 132, 137, 215, 217, 218, 219, 220, 224
degrees, 66, 81, 83, 100, 107, 115, 124, 125, 129, 130, 132
denial, 9, 23, 95, 150, 154, 174, 176
denial of service, 9, 23
department, 15, 39, 48, 93, 109, 182
deployed, 89
designer, 84
designing, 76, 78, 79
detection, 36, 61, 76, 77, 156, 166, 173, 195, 199, 200, 201, 204, 205, 206, 224
developer, 59, 63, 93
developers, 1, 59, 61, 63, 64, 89, 222
development, 52, 59, 60, 61, 63, 64, 67, 99, 100, 112, 117, 136, 140, 144, 156, 160, 165, 181, 199, 221, 228, 229
DevOps, 203
DHS, 123, 198
digital, 1, 2, 11, 18, 28, 34, 52, 53, 54, 83, 84, 87, 99, 100, 101, 102, 104, 105, 113, 116, 122, 127, 131, 141, 181, 211, 220
Digital, 100, 101, 104, 105, 108, 178
digital forensics, 100, 101, 104
digitized, 57
disaster recovery, 166
disclosure, 13, 28, 29, 98
distributed, 9, 23, 153, 160
domain, 8, 136, 160, 203
domains, 67, 107, 135, 136, 138, 139, 205

E

EC, 91, 107, 109, 110, 118, 131, 137
education, 2, 4, 47, 60, 73, 74, 93, 99, 101, 107, 124, 136, 137, 138, 219
Education, 2, 4, 81, 100, 107, 114, 124, 129
electronic, 1, 3, 26, 102, 105
email, 4, 6, 7, 10, 18, 19, 46, 49, 51, 58, 133, 153, 155, 158, 178, 187, 188
emails, 6, 7, 10, 153, 187, 188, 190, 194, 201, 205
employee, 14, 43, 47, 48, 49, 50, 59, 71, 131, 152, 153, 187, 194
encrypt, 79, 85, 126, 151, 156
encrypted, 21, 22, 126, 128, 151, 191, 192, 195, 196
encryption, 16, 103, 118, 121, 122, 123, 126, 127, 128, 155, 171, 173, 195, 196, 219
enforcement, 11, 100, 109, 123, 126, 128, 173
engineer, 62, 67, 101, 125, 220, 231, 232
engineering, 20, 60, 61, 62, 67, 81, 82, 92, 93, 96, 100, 102, 115, 117, 119, 122, 124, 178, 186, 187, 190, 194, 195, 228
engineers, 61, 62, 64, 86, 89
enterprises, 13, 30, 39, 43, 44, 52, 106, 141, 170, 179, 182, 183, 184, 185, 188, 190, 194, 198, 200
entry-level, 66, 67, 73, 80, 81, 84, 100, 129, 131, 133, 212, 217, 218
error, 46, 74, 151, 155, 190, 200
escalation, 48, 151, 152, 175, 176
ethical, 6, 86, 87, 88, 89, 90, 91, 92, 93, 94, 95, 96, 97, 98, 99, 113, 114, 116, 120, 122
Ethical, 40, 67, 85, 87, 91, 93, 98, 216
ethical hacker, 88, 90, 97, 98
evaluation, 96, 107, 114, 141, 142, 143, 144, 198

examinations, 72
examiner, 101
exfiltration, 87
experience, 37, 51, 60, 61, 62, 66, 68, 72, 77, 78, 79, 80, 90, 93, 99, 101, 106, 107, 110, 111, 113, 117, 118, 124, 125, 129, 130, 132, 138, 139, 200, 201, 212, 215, 216, 217
expert, 46, 67, 69, 78, 88, 101, 105, 137, 177, 184, 217, 220, 221
expertise, 32, 60, 62, 66, 73, 74, 75, 78, 79, 82, 83, 87, 89, 98, 110, 112, 117, 119, 120, 126, 129, 139, 215, 216, 220
exploit, 64, 92, 96, 102, 113, 116, 121, 189, 193, 195, 220, 230
exploitation, 7, 13, 120, 156
exploited, 12, 87, 187, 193, 195, 202, 224
exploits, 19, 116, 121, 151
extortion, 6, 11, 12

F

faults, 113
FBI, 123, 126, 188, 189
field, 19, 54, 55, 59, 62, 66, 67, 68, 69, 71, 78, 79, 81, 97, 101, 107, 108, 115, 117, 124, 125, 129, 130, 132, 135, 137, 138, 139, 203, 216, 217, 218, 219
file, 6, 8, 16, 19, 80, 90, 103, 105, 159, 178, 186, 203, 205
financial, 5, 7, 8, 10, 12, 24, 26, 40, 98, 110, 111, 146, 164, 213
firewall, 56, 77, 156, 157, 159, 185
firewalls, 17, 56, 65, 69, 75, 79, 80, 84, 85, 90, 118, 133, 152, 154, 157, 219
firms, 12, 24, 32, 36, 37, 43, 57, 82, 96, 109, 124, 133, 164, 165, 170, 177, 184, 186, 187, 189, 194, 195, 197, 213
Firms, 25

flaws, 57, 64, 80, 87, 96, 113, 119, 152, 156, 174, 175, 177, 178, 187, 189, 198, 206, 219, 225, 226
forensic, 100, 102, 104, 105, 120, 164
forensic specialists, 100
forensics, 99, 100, 101, 102, 104, 105
Forensics, 104
fourth-party, 142
framework, 30, 31, 32, 33, 34, 35, 36, 37, 38, 39, 40, 42, 43, 44, 52, 93
frameworks, 25, 31, 32, 33, 35, 36, 44, 139
fraud, 7, 10, 40, 42, 43, 56, 104, 176, 203, 209
fraudsters, 161, 183
freelance, 93, 97, 98

G

GDPR, 30, 38, 39, 75, 77, 110
GIAC, 103, 108, 118, 131
Golang, 117
good guys, 86, 113, 114
Google, 137, 140, 172, 205, 222
Google's, 172
government, 2, 9, 11, 24, 25, 28, 35, 100, 123, 126, 128, 178
Governments, 2, 100

H

hacker, 6, 12, 19, 20, 21, 22, 56, 57, 73, 86, 87, 88, 89, 90, 91, 93, 94, 95, 96, 97, 98, 99, 116, 162, 180, 186, 187, 230
hackers, 1, 2, 4, 5, 6, 8, 11, 12, 15, 19, 20, 21, 24, 55, 56, 58, 62, 76, 85, 86, 87, 88, 89, 90, 92, 93, 94, 95, 97, 98, 99, 113, 114, 116, 120, 123, 128, 137, 143, 155, 157, 177, 178, 179, 181, 185, 186, 187, 191, 193, 195, 216, 224, 228
Hackers, 8, 11, 19, 22, 57, 155, 193, 210, 214, 223, 225

hacking, 6, 9, 11, 13, 19, 28, 59, 89, 91, 97, 98, 116, 120, 122, 137, 178, 217, 226
handling, 76, 105, 120, 121, 210
harassment, 6
hardware, 3, 4, 17, 18, 82, 95, 102, 103, 104, 132, 140, 150, 151, 154, 168, 181, 224
hazards, 27, 61, 70, 145, 204, 207
healthcare, 21, 25, 26, 33, 35, 165
Healthcare, 38
hijacking, 155, 174, 189
HIPAA, 26, 32, 33, 35, 75, 77
hunters, 89

I

IaaS, 168, 169, 170, 171, 174
IACIS, 103, 108
IACR, 125
IAM, 67, 71
identity, 6, 7, 139, 163, 167, 169, 171
Identity, 10, 71, 139, 173
IEEE, 103, 118
IFCA, 125
illegal, 6, 7, 10, 90, 98, 140
implement, 26, 65, 76, 85, 113, 133, 144, 181, 186, 193
incident, 65, 113, 120, 122, 146, 147, 148, 149, 150, 156, 160, 161, 162, 163, 164, 165, 166, 181, 203, 231
incident response, 65, 122, 146, 161, 162, 163, 164, 165, 166, 203
infections, 20, 53, 153
information, 1, 2, 3, 4, 6, 8, 9, 10, 11, 12, 13, 15, 16, 18, 19, 20, 21, 22, 25, 26, 28, 29, 30, 31, 32, 33, 34, 35, 37, 38, 39, 41, 46, 47, 49, 50, 51, 52, 53, 54, 71, 73, 74, 79, 80, 82, 84, 85, 87, 88, 92, 94, 95, 97, 99, 100, 102, 104, 106, 107, 108, 109, 110, 111, 112, 113, 115, 116, 117, 119, 121, 124, 125, 127, 129, 130, 131, 132, 133, 139, 141, 145, 146, 147, 148, 150, 151, 153, 154, 158, 161, 162, 169, 171, 174, 178, 179, 181, 182, 183, 186, 187, 192, 195, 197, 200, 201, 208, 209, 212, 213, 214, 216, 217, 218, 219, 225, 226, 227
InfoSec, 100, 107, 108, 109, 110, 111, 124, 130, 132
infrastructure, 4, 36, 74, 80, 83, 96, 98, 120, 121, 140, 141, 167, 168, 169, 170, 172, 181, 184, 216
injection, 157, 189, 191, 195, 227
insecure, 21, 155, 174
inspection, 75, 195
integrity, 3, 15, 73, 114, 131, 150, 155
intelligence, 12, 20, 78, 82, 93, 123, 179, 199, 200, 204, 206, 207, 208, 220
internal, 40, 41, 42, 43, 44, 48, 86, 87, 88, 97, 131, 140, 144, 157, 173
internet, 1, 4, 9, 10, 18, 20, 49, 52, 53, 56, 63, 76, 102, 122, 137, 153, 160, 164, 173, 198, 209, 224
Internet, 9, 10, 11, 37, 52, 56, 58, 179, 188, 205
internet-of-things, 63
internship, 138
intrusions, 11, 79
inventions, 113
investigation, 98, 99, 100, 102
Investigation, 101
investigations, 104, 164
investment, 26, 137
investments, 25, 55, 97
iOS, 104, 118, 227
IoT, 2, 58, 63, 102, 179, 206
iPhone, 104
IPS, 75, 118
IRP, 161
ISACA, 37, 108, 109
ISC, 103, 108
ISFCE, 103, 108
ISO, 25, 32, 33, 34, 35, 75, 77, 110
IT, 3, 18, 31, 33, 34, 35, 36, 37, 38, 46, 48, 50, 53, 54, 70, 74, 93, 95,

103, 106, 108, 112, 113, 129, 130, 131, 132, 141, 152, 164, 165, 176, 177, 182, 184, 209, 214, 219

J

Java, 83, 103, 127, 221, 222, 223, 224
Javascript, 72, 79
JavaScript, 224, 225

K

Kali, 118

L

lab, 72, 92, 137
language, 50, 86, 161, 182, 207, 220, 221, 222, 223, 224, 225, 226, 227, 228, 229, 230, 231, 232
launch, 12, 20, 94, 149
Law, 11
laws, 2, 11, 24, 26, 29, 33, 40, 42, 110
leadership, 75, 106, 111, 121, 135, 136, 182
Leadership, 50
Linux, 90, 110, 118, 223, 227
loss, 17, 55, 140, 145, 146, 153, 162, 163, 164, 185, 187

M

machine, 91, 153, 175, 179, 187, 191, 200, 201, 204, 206, 209, 229
macOS, 118, 227
mail, 6, 7, 9
malicious, 1, 21, 85, 86, 91, 95, 113, 156, 159, 163, 178, 181, 186, 187, 191, 193, 205, 207, 209, 229
malware, 20, 69, 85, 102, 140, 149, 153, 154, 159, 160, 174, 178, 186, 187, 188, 189, 190, 192, 193, 203, 204, 205, 206, 208, 220, 223, 224, 231, 232
Malware, 20, 38, 69, 153, 186
management, 32, 34, 36, 38, 39, 42, 50, 65, 66, 67, 69, 70, 75, 79, 82, 86, 92, 93, 96, 97, 100, 106, 110, 111, 113, 134, 135, 136, 139, 141, 142, 160, 163, 165, 166, 167, 169, 171, 172, 189, 192, 193, 197, 223
Management, 27, 38, 68, 69, 71, 135, 139, 168, 173
Managing, 71
master's, 66, 100, 107, 117, 124, 125, 215, 217
measures, 3, 26, 27, 31, 32, 36, 52, 55, 56, 64, 65, 69, 70, 76, 77, 83, 85, 87, 90, 95, 120, 121, 146, 176, 179, 181, 183, 191, 213, 217
messages, 6, 7, 10, 154, 158, 186
metadata, 103
Metasploit, 93, 118
Microsoft, 62, 169
migrations, 78
military, 9, 81, 82, 121, 128
mitigation, 84, 90, 121, 183, 186, 193, 195, 217, 231
MitM, 154, 155
ML, 144, 179, 203
mobile, 1, 3, 4, 46, 99, 102, 104, 105, 118, 120, 132, 140, 179, 222, 228
modeling, 94, 95, 119, 139
models, 25, 168, 205
money, 7, 11, 12, 21, 24, 25, 53, 54, 56, 58, 59, 143, 162, 178, 188, 221
monitoring, 55, 75, 77, 133, 140, 152, 173, 175, 176, 217
multifactor, 39, 76, 156, 181
MySQL, 227

N

national, 2, 9, 96, 98, 121, 198
Nessus, and others, 118
Net, 103

Netsparker, 93
network, 1, 3, 4, 6, 8, 10, 19, 20, 21, 22, 23, 52, 53, 55, 61, 62, 65, 67, 68, 69, 72, 73, 75, 76, 80, 81, 82, 83, 85, 87, 89, 91, 92, 94, 99, 102, 106, 113, 115, 116, 117, 118, 120, 121, 125, 127, 128, 129, 131, 133, 134, 140, 142, 145, 146, 148, 151, 152, 154,155, 156, 157, 158, 169, 171, 173, 178, 180, 185, 186, 192, 196, 199, 201, 204, 205, 206, 207, 210, 212, 216, 220, 229, 232
networking, 6, 10, 62, 65, 69, 72, 78, 104, 109, 110, 168, 216
networks, 1, 3, 6, 9, 11, 17, 18, 35, 65, 69, 71, 72, 76, 79, 80, 82, 85, 88, 90, 94, 97, 102, 114, 119, 123, 126, 132, 133, 134, 136, 149, 157, 158, 179, 180, 181, 201, 207, 208, 210, 211, 219, 226, 232
NIST, 19, 25, 33, 35, 36, 38, 44, 110
NMAP, 118
Node.js, 72, 79
non-technical, 75, 119
NSA, 123, 126
NUIX, 103

O

objectives, 2, 13, 31, 37, 40, 42, 43, 61, 63, 105, 141, 142, 147, 230
offensive, 65, 69, 85, 86, 87, 88, 89, 92, 93, 98, 116, 119
online, 3, 4, 5, 6, 10, 11, 15, 18, 56, 57, 58, 68, 72, 82, 93, 120, 135, 141, 149, 160, 178, 181, 185, 198, 200, 222, 224
operating, 32, 84, 90, 91, 102, 104, 113, 118, 119, 121, 128, 169, 185, 191, 192, 196, 222, 223, 228
operational, 31, 32, 37, 38, 43, 103, 108, 112, 130, 136, 198
operations, 11, 29, 39, 40, 41, 43, 47, 51, 54, 59, 60, 67, 99, 106, 110, 113, 116, 119, 120, 126, 140, 142, 150, 157, 160, 166, 167, 173, 182, 186, 224
Operations, 40, 97
Organizations, 2, 32, 44, 65, 74, 141, 152, 156, 157, 158, 162
OSCP, 68, 91, 108, 118, 121
OSI, 75
OSINT, 115, 119
OWASP, 118

P

PaaS, 168, 169, 170, 171, 175
password, 20, 22, 76, 77, 103, 151, 155, 156, 159, 161, 193, 197
passwords, 4, 10, 15, 22, 46, 49, 59, 156, 190, 193, 195, 197, 209, 212
patch, 87, 163
pen, 86, 91, 98, 114, 115, 117, 118, 119, 121, 227
penetration, 62, 65, 69, 70, 82, 86, 87, 92, 93, 112, 113, 114, 115, 116, 117, 118, 119, 120, 121, 157, 216, 230
Penetration, 38, 113, 114, 217
Perl, 72, 79, 83, 228, 229
permission, 8, 88, 215
personal, 2, 5, 7, 10, 11, 18, 29, 30, 32, 39, 140, 158, 162, 181, 193, 196, 210, 227
phishing, 12, 19, 20, 22, 48, 49, 59, 153, 174, 178, 186, 187, 188, 190, 194, 205, 208, 225
PHP, 83, 103, 225, 226, 232
plans, 17, 42, 92, 134, 148, 162, 166, 181
PlayStation, 160
policy, 15, 30, 32, 49, 111, 192, 196, 212
position, 24, 48, 60, 66, 67, 69, 77, 78, 80, 90, 93, 94, 106, 107, 117, 129, 131, 217, 218, 220
potential risks, 142, 203

Powershell, 117
PowerShell, 72, 79
privacy, 2, 3, 24, 28, 39, 155
private, 2, 4, 20, 21, 24, 29, 35, 36, 46, 81, 82, 85, 114, 116, 128, 151, 167, 170, 178, 180, 183, 186, 187
privileges, 3, 151, 152, 197
procedures, 3, 25, 29, 30, 32, 34, 39, 41, 43, 84, 105, 111, 119, 120, 133, 139, 147, 166, 182, 193
product, 13, 60, 61, 63, 64, 75, 185
professionals, 32, 40, 66, 67, 79, 80, 81, 82, 83, 84, 104, 109, 129, 134, 192, 213, 215, 217, 218, 220, 221, 222, 224
Professionals, 59, 66, 67, 97, 101, 216
profiles, 6, 20, 208
program, 33, 34, 44, 48, 66, 110, 112, 141, 142, 156, 160, 169, 197, 216, 218, 229
programming, 60, 62, 83, 103, 115, 117, 124, 126, 127, 128, 174, 220, 221, 222, 223, 224, 225, 226, 227, 228, 229, 230, 231, 232
programming language, 222, 223, 228, 232
programs, 8, 34, 49, 50, 62, 71, 92, 100, 108, 111, 115, 118, 126, 130, 131, 133, 137, 189, 191, 192, 194, 195, 196, 213, 214, 217, 218, 223, 224
Project, 75, 79
protocols, 48, 85, 100, 114, 118, 128, 134, 165, 166
providers, 140, 142, 188
purple, 86, 89
Python, 72, 79, 103, 117, 127, 223, 224, 228, 229

Q

qualifications, 68, 69, 70, 72, 79, 124, 127, 130, 137

R

ransomware, 1, 11, 12, 13, 21, 134, 153, 162, 178, 185, 186, 187, 192, 196, 205, 208
Ransomware, 21, 82, 187, 192
records, 2, 7, 12, 98, 113, 148, 160, 181
recoverable, 104
recovery, 17, 34, 36, 134, 140, 143, 148, 149, 166, 196
Red, 86, 120
remote, 164, 189
reporting, 39, 40, 42, 43, 109, 122
reports, 43, 97, 219, 228
requirements, 26, 27, 28, 30, 31, 33, 34, 38, 39, 42, 44, 52, 63, 67, 77, 78, 102, 106, 107, 110, 111, 117, 127, 129, 131, 198, 222, 231
researchers, 89, 198, 203
resources, 11, 38, 40, 49, 54, 72, 93, 107, 108, 109, 111, 131, 135, 139, 141, 142, 143, 148, 149, 156, 161, 170, 173, 182, 209, 227
risk, 1, 2, 5, 28, 31, 36, 37, 38, 39, 41, 42, 44, 53, 56, 67, 70, 71, 78, 85, 89, 95, 96, 97, 110, 112, 134, 136, 138, 141, 142, 143, 144, 147, 150, 152, 164, 172, 182, 183, 184, 185, 189, 193, 198, 200, 201, 204, 231
routers, 58, 154
Ruby, 72, 79, 228
rules, 24, 25, 29, 41, 42, 77, 133, 144, 146, 147, 165, 196, 205

S

SaaS, 168, 169, 170, 171, 176
safeguard, 18, 26, 39, 49, 69, 72, 85, 91, 141, 142, 144, 152, 172, 179, 196, 207, 219
safeguarding, 1, 2, 107, 146, 167, 169
SANS, 37, 108, 110, 118, 131

science, 62, 66, 81, 90, 92, 100, 117, 122, 124, 129, 130, 132, 208, 217, 218, 220
scripting, 72, 79, 156, 175, 224
SDLC, 110
security, 1, 2, 3, 4, 12, 14, 15, 16, 17, 18, 20, 24, 25, 26, 27, 28, 29, 31, 32, 33, 34, 35, 36, 37, 38, 39, 44, 46, 47, 48, 49, 51, 52, 53, 54, 55, 56, 57, 58, 59, 60, 61, 62, 63, 64, 65, 66, 67, 68, 69, 70, 71, 72, 73, 74, 75, 76, 77, 78, 79, 80, 81, 82, 83, 84, 85, 86, 87, 88, 89, 91, 92, 93, 94, 95, 96, 97, 98, 99, 100, 102, 104, 106, 107, 108, 109, 110, 111, 112, 114, 115, 116, 117, 118, 119, 120, 121, 122, 123, 124, 125, 127, 128, 129, 130, 131, 132, 133, 134, 135, 136, 137, 138, 139, 140, 141, 142, 146, 147, 148, 150, 152, 154, 156, 157, 159, 160, 161, 162, 163, 164, 165, 166, 167, 168, 169, 170, 171, 172, 173, 174, 175, 176, 178, 179, 180, 181, 182, 183, 184, 188, 189, 191, 192, 193, 194, 195, 196, 197, 198, 199, 200, 201, 202, 203, 204, 206, 207, 208, 210, 211, 212, 213, 214, 216, 217, 218, 219, 220, 221, 222, 223, 224, 225, 227, 228, 229, 231, 232
Security, 3, 27, 30, 32, 33, 37, 38, 44, 46, 54, 57, 62, 63, 65, 67, 68, 69, 70, 72, 73, 74, 76, 77, 82, 83, 89, 91, 94, 95, 96, 103, 106, 108, 109, 111, 118, 128, 131, 133, 137, 138, 139, 140, 155, 168, 171, 172, 173, 174, 175, 176, 185, 191, 198, 204, 214, 215, 216, 220, 224, 230
security administrators, 131, 133
security architects, 65, 68, 69
security architectures, 70, 168, 172
security experts, 31, 76, 86, 98, 106, 211, 213, 214, 217, 221, 224
senior, 36, 50, 97, 106, 115, 117, 120, 121, 136, 160, 182

sensitive, 1, 3, 7, 9, 15, 19, 21, 25, 49, 52, 98, 113, 114, 123, 126, 127, 143, 146, 150, 151, 152, 157, 175, 178, 179, 181, 185, 187, 189, 190, 191, 196, 197, 201, 209, 219
server, 21, 59, 92, 94, 133, 148, 154, 156, 158, 161, 164, 186, 225, 226
servers, 1, 3, 17, 90, 105, 154, 157, 158
SIEM, 75, 206
simulated, 48, 49, 87, 88, 93
simulation, 48, 88
skills, 5, 25, 57, 62, 69, 70, 72, 74, 78, 83, 84, 89, 90, 97, 101, 104, 107, 108, 110, 113, 115, 116, 118, 127, 130, 132, 135, 136, 214, 215, 218, 219, 220, 230, 231
small, 1, 24, 53, 104, 131, 164, 177, 182, 183, 184, 185, 186, 187, 188, 189, 192, 193, 194, 195, 196, 197, 198
SOAR, 206
social, 6, 18, 20, 49, 51, 82, 93, 96, 98, 119, 178, 186, 187, 190, 194, 195, 226, 227
social engineering, 20, 93, 94, 178, 186, 190, 194
software, 3, 7, 8, 17, 18, 57, 59, 60, 61, 62, 63, 64, 67, 69, 71, 79, 82, 84, 85, 87, 93, 99, 100, 102, 103, 104, 105, 112, 117, 121, 128, 132, 139, 140, 150, 151, 152, 153, 154, 155, 159, 167, 168, 169, 170, 176, 178, 181, 185, 186, 187, 188, 192, 197, 199, 204, 206, 219, 222, 231, 232
solutions, 1, 17, 20, 36, 52, 53, 57, 60, 74, 78, 79, 128, 171, 174, 184, 185, 192, 195, 197, 199, 206, 208, 209, 231
SP, 33, 35, 36
spam, 6, 201, 205
Spear, 20, 153
specialists, 2, 43, 57, 87, 94, 99, 100, 101, 102, 105, 130, 134, 212

specialty, 93
spoofing, 6, 7
spyware, 152, 153
SQL, 22, 157, 191, 227
SSH, 155
SSL, 59, 75
standards, 25, 26, 27, 28, 29, 32, 33, 34, 35, 36, 38, 40, 42, 44, 75, 77, 89, 98, 110, 112, 116, 137, 145, 161, 172, 173
storage, 3, 34, 82, 139, 158, 161, 168, 179, 191, 196
strategies, 13, 54, 85, 89, 94, 120, 121, 122, 134, 140, 141, 148, 161, 162, 178, 180, 186, 194, 231
susceptible, 177, 184, 227
SWGDE, 101, 108
Swift, 227, 228
synchronization, 179
system, 1, 4, 7, 11, 13, 14, 18, 19, 21, 23, 27, 28, 34, 40, 41, 42, 43, 44, 50, 53, 54, 55, 56, 67, 71, 76, 85, 88, 91, 95, 96, 113, 114, 115, 119, 120, 121, 127, 128, 133, 134, 147, 150, 151, 152, 154, 155, 159, 160, 161, 171, 178, 179, 185, 187, 189, 191, 192, 195, 196, 197, 202, 203, 207, 208, 220, 222, 223, 229, 232
systems, 1, 3, 6, 11, 13, 21, 28, 29, 38, 43, 46, 53, 54, 55, 58, 60, 64, 71, 73, 79, 80, 84, 87, 88, 90, 91, 92, 96, 97, 102, 104, 112, 113, 114, 116, 118, 119, 120, 123, 125, 126, 127, 128, 129, 131, 132, 133, 136, 139, 140, 141, 147, 148, 149, 151, 156, 158, 159, 160, 169, 173, 179, 190, 193, 194, 195, 196, 197, 198, 199, 200, 202, 203, 206, 207, 208, 209, 216, 223, 224, 228, 229, 232

T

targets, 4, 13, 24, 56, 58, 91, 181, 184

TCP, 224
team, 48, 53, 57, 60, 61, 63, 64, 69, 78, 86, 87, 89, 93, 95, 97, 98, 99, 106, 133, 134, 145, 147, 149, 162, 208, 220
technical, 5, 13, 38, 50, 61, 64, 74, 75, 78, 86, 89, 90, 92, 100, 103, 108, 112, 119, 120, 121, 123, 125, 126, 129, 130, 132, 135, 136, 137, 138, 182, 198, 215, 219
technician, 101, 216, 217
technique, 3, 22, 48, 151, 157, 200
techniques, 3, 16, 57, 64, 68, 74, 87, 89, 92, 102, 105, 113, 116, 120, 127, 128, 140, 147, 155, 167, 172, 178, 186, 194, 201, 206, 210, 224, 230
technological, 37, 90, 128, 177
technologies, 16, 52, 79, 85, 119, 120, 128, 132, 144, 154, 181, 189, 195, 197, 224, 231
technology, 1, 3, 5, 6, 11, 13, 18, 33, 52, 59, 60, 70, 73, 74, 79, 82, 92, 96, 100, 102, 110, 125, 126, 129, 130, 132, 133, 136, 141, 179, 180, 212, 216, 218, 219, 222
tester, 62, 86, 91, 113, 115, 216
testers, 86, 98, 113, 114, 115, 116, 117, 119, 227, 230
testing, 48, 62, 64, 65, 67, 69, 70, 82, 93, 101, 112, 113, 114, 115, 117, 118, 119, 120, 194
Testing, 38, 214
threat, 1, 19, 51, 52, 61, 84, 86, 93, 94, 95, 96, 119, 139, 141, 142, 143, 151, 152, 154, 157, 167, 173, 183, 193, 199, 201, 204, 206, 208, 209, 220, 231
Threat modeling, 95
threats, 3, 6, 19, 47, 48, 50, 51, 60, 61, 63, 64, 68, 70, 74, 82, 95, 96, 97, 112, 133, 134, 139, 140, 142, 143, 145, 147, 148, 149, 152, 163, 174, 183, 185, 186, 187, 189, 190, 198, 199, 200, 204, 208, 209, 211

TLS, 155
tools, 3, 17, 30, 47, 51, 54, 60, 75, 87, 91, 93, 102, 113, 118, 119, 121, 136, 152, 162, 167, 174, 179, 183, 193, 201, 214, 219, 224, 230, 231, 232
training, 47, 48, 49, 50, 59, 62, 68, 71, 73, 77, 78, 80, 81, 84, 96, 99, 101, 103, 107, 108, 109, 124, 126, 129, 130, 137, 194, 217, 218, 220
transaction, 12, 203
transactions, 18, 53
Turing, 200
Turing test, 200

U

unauthorized, 3, 7, 8, 16, 25, 39, 71, 105, 128, 139, 140, 150, 151, 156, 158, 176, 189, 227
unethical, 90, 98
unpatched, 187
unprotected, 21
updating, 84
username, 20, 76

V

verifications, 41
virtual, 73, 91, 118, 176, 180, 189
virtualization, 110
virtually, 32, 76
virus, 1, 8, 19, 20, 22, 53, 161, 187, 201
VM, 175
VPNs, 75, 155, 180
VTA, 94, 96

VTC, 189
vulnerabilities, 31, 60, 62, 87, 91, 93, 95, 96, 97, 113, 116, 120, 121, 134, 141, 142, 143, 146, 147, 156, 172, 178, 179, 183, 189, 190, 191, 192, 193, 198, 199, 207, 212, 214, 216, 230
vulnerability, 4, 70, 71, 86, 93, 94, 96, 112, 113, 117, 121, 122, 151, 170, 171, 176, 189, 190, 191, 193, 194, 198, 200, 227
vulnerable, 64, 89, 94, 183, 185, 209

W

weakness, 116, 187
weaknesses, 86, 88, 91, 92, 94, 96, 142, 147, 175, 176, 179, 185, 190, 194, 216
web, 21, 99, 113, 114, 115, 116, 119, 121, 156, 157, 159, 179, 191, 204, 209, 216, 224, 225, 226, 227, 229
website, 6, 9, 21, 22, 53, 87, 109, 124, 153, 178, 186, 187, 209, 226, 232
websites, 6, 8, 9, 18, 21, 51, 68, 88, 155, 156, 160, 178, 190, 193, 197, 209, 225, 226, 227, 228, 232
Whitehat, 85
Windows, 90, 118, 159, 223
wireless, 90, 116, 119, 120, 133
Wireshark, 118
workstations, 90

Z

zero-day, 174, 206, 207

www.ingramcontent.com/pod-product-compliance
Lightning Source LLC
Chambersburg PA
CBHW052345220526
45465CB00003BA/970